FURTWÄNGLER RECALLED

FURTWÄNGLER
RECALLED

EDITED WITH AN INTRODUCTION BY
DANIEL GILLIS

John de Graff Inc.
Tuckahoe, New York

Library of Congress   Catalog Card Number: 65-23852

© 1965   Atlantis Verlag AG Zürich

PRINTED IN SWITZERLAND

INTRODUCTION

In his later years, Wilhelm Furtwängler spoke of writing his autobiography; he died before he could begin it. The greater part of
his letters and essays will soon be accessible in English; but for
memories of the man himself, of his art and his genius, we must
turn to those who were close to the musical world in which he
moved.

The following pages come from the pens of three generations of
writers — conductors, opera singers, composers, pianists, concertmasters, cellists, violinists, correspondents, critics who knew Furtwängler only on the podium, and orchestral musicians who played
under him for decades. These writers have tried to express what Furtwängler was, what he meant, and what he gave them. Their memories will enrich those of British audiences which enjoyed his visits
to England for thirty years; and the American musical public, unable
to hear him conduct after 1927, will sense what it has missed.

I wish to express my gratitude to Frau Elisabeth Furtwängler for
her cooperation, to the many writers who answered my requests
for material, and to those whose previously published works are
here reproduced with permission. For his assistance, I express my
thanks to Dr. Martin Hürlimann, whose volume *Wilhelm Furtwängler
im Urteil seiner Zeit* served as a model for the present one. And I
must not forget to thank Miss Mary A. Smith for having introduced
me to Furtwängler's recordings so many years ago.

Munich, May 1964   *Daniel Gillis*

Von Herzen — möge es wieder zu Herzen gehen

BEETHOVEN, MISSA SOLEMNIS

Wilhelm Furtwängler

born in Berlin, January 25, 1886
died in Baden-Baden, November 30, 1954

I

Messages to Elisabeth Furtwängler

To the Furtwängler family

I was deeply moved when I learned of the death of the great artist. Allow me to express my condolence from afar. I should like to have attended the funeral ceremonies, for I know that the deceased felt the same friendship toward me as I toward him. In our youth, at the home of Curtius in Strasbourg, we were introduced and took an instant liking to each other. Only rarely were we able to meet again. It was a treat for us when we did meet. It was a silent friendship. Each of us knew that the other followed his progress with interest. This understanding without words we both felt as something beautiful. And now he, the younger, has departed from the world, after a splendidly fulfilled work. With others we gratefully recall the precious hours when he gave us his splendid music. In gratitude we remain united with him. And we who were privileged to know him remember not only the great artist but also the dear and noble man. In a time of servility he was a man unbowed, and he bore persecution with dignity and courage. As a man he has had great meaning for his time. We thank him too for remaining true to himself.

I write to you in the midst of preparations for my trip to Lambaréné in three days. I find myself in a state of deep fatigue and do not know how I shall complete the work yet to be done, how I shall carry on at all. So I cannot consider speaking on the radio for the memorial ceremonies. My grief for him now must remain silent, as our friendship has been. I enjoyed our most wonderful hours together many years ago in Zürich, when he was conducting some concerts there and I was giving a lecture.

With kindest regards, devotedly yours,
ALBERT SCHWEITZER

That your husband's illness, which his friends and admirers followed with worried hearts, has now resulted in his untimely death, moves countless hearts with sorrow, yet also with lonely gratitude. In the sphere of music he was not only the great mediator but also the truly creative interpreter who faithfully reproduced the composer's intentions from the richness of his own soul.

THEODOR HEUSS

On the occasion of the death of your husband I express my
deeply felt condolence to you and to your family. German musical
life loses in the deceased one of its most distinguished personalities. Through his artistic renown, extending far beyond the
frontiers of Germany, Doctor Wilhelm Furtwängler has won for
himself an enduring remembrance.

ADENAUER, Chancellor

Tokyo, December 1, 1954

Dear Elisabeth,

I felt at once the disaster that has struck you, which touches the hearts of musicians everywhere with such sorrow. When you read these words from so far away, I hope you will feel that I am with you, sympathizing with the sorrow in your heart and realizing that music is now deprived of its greatest interpreter.

No consolation is possible, other than the memories our respect, admiration, and affection will always cherish. For me, a light has gone out which will never be rekindled. But his example will live on as one of the greatest inspirations of my life; and I shall always be grateful for the friendship he gave me, the enrichment each of his interpretations gave me, the faith and truth he loved.

I embrace you tenderly, dear Elisabeth, and your children, and send you all my love.

PIERRE FOURNIER

Dear Frau Furtwängler,

The news of your husband's death has deeply shaken us. It seems impossible that it can be true, and that this unforgettable artist and man is actually no longer among us. I feel as if Germany has lost the very foundations of her artistic life.

In these, your hardest hours, our thoughts are with you and your children. Beyond these, only the knowledge of what your husband has meant and always will mean for Art—in an incomparable way—can give consolation for your irreparable loss.

May this realization help you in your sorrow.

Your devoted
HERBERT and LISELOTTE GRAF

1   Court Conductor in Mannheim, c. 1915

2   Vienna, 1930

Madame,

What can one say to you? We are all heartbroken, and we understand your inexpressible sorrow. Words are of no avail. Allow me simply to tell you with what respect I think of your sorrow, with what emotion I recall the memory of the ingenious artist you lament, and how much I thank him for all the countless joys, so great and so dear, that he has given us. Forgive me for these words, which come to you from all my heart.

NADIA BOULANGER

Stuttgart, December 5, 1954

Today, dear Frau Furtwängler, for the first time I am able to tell you that our thoughts are with you in pain and sorrow. I was so shaken by the news of the death of Wilhelm Furtwängler that I simply could not write. And yet whatever one writes is too poor to begin to touch your pain and the magnitude of the loss which you and your family, we ourselves, and the entire artistic world have suffered.

Allow me to give you my hand in silence, in deep gratitude for all the great artist has given me since I was privileged to hear him for the first time in Berlin so many years ago. I have admired the great artist and loved the man. I am proud that I was close to him in hard times, and that he called me his friend. Unforgettable were those hours in your home, and when he came to us in Berlin and Stuttgart . . .

Our thoughts are with you in deep sympathy,

Your

RUDOLF PECHEL

Lisbon, December 6, 1954

Dear Frau Furtwängler,

Please forgive me if I burden you with these lines, but the death of Dr. Furtwängler has come as too great a shock for me to remain silent. The musical world has lost in him the greatest conductor of all time. You know how much I loved and admired your husband with all my heart. This wonderful artist will be my ideal all my life: this is my only wish.

Here in Lisbon a short commemoration was held for Dr. Furtwängler during my concert. After the memorial address, we played the *Air in G* of Bach. With this I tried to send from afar a last greeting to the great artist.

With all my heart, in sorrow,
your devoted, grateful
KARL MÜNCHINGER

Dear Frau Furtwängler,

You can never know how painful the news of your husband's death was for me. I owe to him my first great musical impressions, and to the end his concerts were among the most beautiful and most sublime I have ever heard. During his lifetime, it was never possible for me to express to him my boundless love and enthusiasm, not even remotely, and I am afraid that even now I can only express them very imperfectly to you. What fire, what high inspiration lived in this man! It is inconceivable that he has passed from us. We are all poorer now.

How grateful I am, that I was privileged to hear him so often, especially during the past summer! I shall never forget the Schubert concert in Vienna, the *Freischütz* and *Don Giovanni* in Salzburg, the Bruckner *Seventh* and Beethoven *Ninth* in Lucerne. There was a blooming and streaming richness in his music such as I have never witnessed before, even in him. But among my happiest memories is the experience of having played twice under him, of having been near him twice.

All of us who were privileged to know and hear him share your pain.

With deepest sympathy, your
PAUL BADURA-SKODA

New York, December 14, 1954

Dear Mrs. Furtwängler,

Coming over by boat from Norway I just heard the sad news, and I want you to know how terribly I feel about the passing of the greatest conductor and to me the favorite. I was never so happy as when I had the privilege to sing under Dr. Furtwängler's direction, and our last time together during the recording of *Tristan* will stand out in my memory for all time.

Please, accept my deepest sympathy.

Yours very sincerely,
KIRSTEN FLAGSTAD

Hamburg, December 20, 1954

Dear Frau Furtwängler,

The news of your husband's death reached me in Brussels, but today is the first moment of peace at home that I have had to express to you personally our deepest sympathy. The loss is infinitely cruel for you as for the world of music. We feel that with Wilhelm Furtwängler an epoch in musical life has ended and become history. When I was privileged to hear him conduct the *Ninth* again last summer in Bayreuth, I sensed that lonely greatness in him, and could only wish that he might remain with us for many years to come. God has willed otherwise, and so only his memory remains with us, eternally. I am grateful to a rare, kind fate that I was privileged to be so close to him in his last years. I shall never forget him, and his spiritual character, his heartfelt approach to music, remain for me an obligation and ideal.

Sending you our deepest consolations,

I remain devotedly,
JOSEPH KEILBERTH

Dear Frau Furtwängler,

When the unbelievable, painful news reached me, with the many writers who spoke and wrote at that time I hoped that the sorrow would gradually develop into lasting and grateful humility, and that it would thus be easier for me to write to you later. But the more often I am forced to realize that the Master, for whom I proudly felt a son's devotion, is no longer with us, the more frightening become our abandonment and the terrible emptiness which all of us who revered his art must feel. Deeply moved, I express my sympathy to you now. Some of us imagine that we have been personally close to him. But who can ever know what you have lost?

His birthday tomorrow will be an especially hard day for you. Allow me simply to offer you my hand in silence—and to say only this: the few years since that rainy day in Salzburg when I first met him and sang under him—years when I was privileged to receive from him leadership, recognition, and the great legacy of a spiritual mission—were decisive for my life. I shall always be grateful for them.

DIETRICH FISCHER-DIESKAU

II

ERNEST ANSERMET

Memorial Broadcast, Geneva, December 1, 1954

THE death of Furtwängler comes as such a shock to me that I find it difficult to put into words all that it has made me feel. For to my mind he was the most genuine, the most searching, and—to summarize all my thoughts—the greatest interpreter of the Classics in our century. He leaves us now, yet we should have needed him for many years to come.

There have appeared in our musical life some currents of new ideas, of new ways of seeing and feeling which are profoundly disturbing. And we could not help but notice in opposition to these Furtwängler's approach to music, which arose from a long tradition, a true kinship with the works he interpreted, and his deeply mature awareness of their meaning, gained through experience and meditation—an approach which we could consider as a norm. The kind of opposition resulting from this approach of Furtwängler's, which was different from that of other famous interpreters of his time, has hindered the public in these last years from appreciating him in his true measure. He suffered much from this because he knew exactly what he was doing and what he had to communicate. His experience, of course, was evident. The critics debated him, yet at the very moment his performances began, the public—the real public—was overwhelmed. Some critics reproached him for remaining too confined to the Classical repertory, others for giving interpretations which did not conform to tradition. But what is it that matters: the works or the tradition? Many did not realize that precisely what gave substance to his interpretations was a vision renewed, deepened and enriched by long experience with these works, a vision bringing together what had already been explored, giving to it a new synthesis, and breathing life into the Classics. Does Laurence Olivier interpret Hamlet as tradition would have it done? And why should Furtwängler have dedicated himself to those works less moulded to his genius than the Classics, when he brought to us from the Classics a vision renewed, whose secret was his alone?

After the war he was a victim of political prejudices of a revolting injustice, for he was absolutely independent of politics, owed nothing to it, had suffered himself from the Nazi régime, was in constant struggle with Nazi leaders, and in those years particularly difficult for him displayed a most commendable and courageous attitude, the attitude of a true messenger of culture.

It would have been better if Furtwängler had lived long enough to see these circumstances dissolved through time, and to feel himself justly recognized. Fate did not permit it. He has passed suddenly and leaves his friends inconsolable. But he has left indelible impressions with those who heard him; he left some writings, and his last volume, *Ton und Wort*, contains pages which will be most rewarding for future generations pondering the meaning of music. He left too some musical compositions which might be disconcerting to the ears of the moderns, but whose true worth, let us hope, will one day be recognized.

From the home of our Orchestra, for which he had only the deepest friendship, on whose podium he gave concerts we shall never forget, I address to his memory the homage of my most fervent admiration, certain that I express at the same time the admiration of our world of music.

CLAUDIA CASSIDY

Memories of Furtwängler, a Great and Tragic Man of Music
The Chicago Daily Tribune, December 1, 1954

Music lost a giant when Wilhelm Furtwängler died. His was the noblest Beethoven I have known, the most revealing Bruckner, in the realm of Mozart the most truly magical *The Magic Flute*. Ironical that Chicago was to have heard such an artist for the first time at three Allied Arts concerts with the Berlin Philharmonic, booked for March in Orchestra Hall. For it was "artists", some of them worthy of the word without quotation marks, whose refusal to appear under his direction caused Furtwängler's withdrawal as guest conductor of the Chicago Symphony Orchestra for what must have been eight indelible weeks in the season of 1949–50.

My first inkling of that boycott came in a secret telephone call from a pianist of the highest rank, obviously under pressure and asking what to do. What did I know of Furtwängler's political record? Nothing, I said. I know what interests me. He is a great conductor. Even recordings prove that. A week or two later the boycott burst into print, the orchestra board got nervous, and Furtwängler withdrew.

How great our loss, how curious the cause, I knew more about when the summer of 1949 took me to Salzburg. I saw the tall, quiet man around whom controversies raged, the man so revered that at a Sunday morning concert those who could not buy tickets for the Festspielhaus waited outside until the doors were opened at the end of the performance, then crowded in, just to applaud. I knew, because I heard it, that he understood and communicated the glory of music. His *Fidelio* was light to banish darkness and truth to shame the lie.

Because of Claire Dux, now Mrs. Hans von der Marwitz, I met him quietly, over coffee. No questions were put. But he made up his mind in my favor. He said: "Is there anything I could tell you that you would like to know?" So we met and talked for hours, finding an interpreter unnecessary, and official documents underscored what I already knew, for I am Irish enough to put more faith in such a face and such music. The *Tribune* printed that interview, a long one, Sunday, September 4, 1949. Later, a letter from his "Emperor" villa in Clarens, Switzerland, thanked the *Tribune* for stating his case.

It was to me a simple, tragic case of a man in high position who felt that his place was with his people. "It would have been much easier to emigrate", he told me, "but there had to be a spiritual center of integrity for all the good and real Germans who had to stay behind. I felt that a really great work of music was a stronger and more essential contradiction of the spirit of Buchenwald and Auschwitz than words could be".

Remembering the *Fidelio*, the matchless Beethoven *Ninth* with which he reopened Bayreuth in 1951, I know that he believed this to be true, and that many Germans and Austrians took strength from his conviction. Though Berlin born, he was a Salzburg, not a Bayreuth man. He found Bayreuth, comparatively, stiff and cold. But though I always heard him with the Vienna Philharmonic, which he loved, he told me, "The Berlin Philharmonic is my right arm". It will be welcome if it comes without him, that Berlin Philharmonic due here on March 11, 12, and 13. The likely replacement is a famous conductor, Herbert von Karajan. But it would be a replacement. For in the realm of the great there is only one of a kind. And Furtwängler is gone.

NEVILLE CARDUS

Furtwängler: An Appreciation
The Manchester Guardian, December 2, 1954

F<small>URTWÄNGLER</small> was almost the last of the German post-Wagner romantic school of music: only Klemperer now survives. For Bruno Walter, though a product of the German romantic tradition and rooted in the nineteenth century, has assimilated an Austrian urbanity which would have been alien to Furt-wängler's style and temperament. Furtwängler conducted in a manner exactly opposed to the Toscanini objectivity: in plainer words, he did not regard the printed notes of the score as a final statement, but rather as so many symbols of an imaginative conception, ever changing and always to be felt and realized subjectively. His variations and tempo often irritated musicians who, in increasing numbers during a period of anti-romanticism, persuaded themselves to believe in music as an arrangement of patterns conveying no emotion or meaning reducible to terms or language related to merely human or egoistical significance.

Furtwängler, a born and superbly equipped musician, was no more capable than Wagner of reacting to music as a thing complete in itself; he sought for the man behind the style; indeed he sought, or seemed to seek, to expose the nerve center. His interpretations of the classic composers were definitely Wagnerian; or post-Wagnerian, stimulating dramatic as well as musical values. He was consequently not a happy conductor in the comedy of Mozart; he was never visited by the comic spirit; he was Echt Deutsch. But as recently as the Salzburg Festival of last summer he conducted a stupendous performance of *Don Giovanni*.

31

More than any conductor of our time, he was Faustian; his faults were the signs of his restless idealism, his impatience with routine and formula. Often as I watched this lean, lonely man quivering the whole of his body as he directed his orchestra, I remembered the lines "Es irrt der Mensch, so lang er strebt". To Furtwängler, truth of musical interpretation came not only from deep study and culture but as much from aesthetic experience and by ordeal of trial and error of the spirit. Not since Nikisch, of whom he was a disciple, has a greater personal interpreter of orchestral and opera music than Furtwängler been heard; his penetration into the germ cell, the blood stream, the nervous system, and the brain center of *Tristan* and *Parsifal* was absolute and consummate; it is not likely that we shall ever hear the intense equal of Furtwängler's Wagner interpretations. Lack of geniality kept him outside the warmest spaces of *Meistersinger*. Last August his conducting of the *Ninth Symphony* of Beethoven was truly noble. He has died too soon, at the period of an artist's maturity. He certainly was an artist; and not all conductors are that.

3, 4   Rehearsal in Vienna, 1944

5   After his last *Ninth* at Bayreuth, 1954

LEO BLECH

Memorial Broadcast, RIAS Berlin, December 7, 1954

Wɪʟʜᴇʟᴍ Furtwängler has passed away. What could one say that the pens of greater writers than I have not already written? He united in his art humility and sovereign power—humility before the composition and sovereign power before his orchestras. With him the guiding spirit of German conducting has passed away.

KARL BÖHM

Memorial Broadcast, RIAS Berlin, December 7, 1954

In deep sorrow I stand at the bier of the man I was privileged to call my friend for nearly twenty years. As his colleague in Vienna and Salzburg, I can well judge what the whole musical world loses in him. In his music he possessed such spiritual power of suggestion that it convinced even those who sometimes held different views of interpretation. He was himself creative as he re-created the score. Who will conduct the Passacaglia of the Brahms *Fourth* or the adagio of a Bruckner or Beethoven symphony after him?

The Vienna State Opera, the Vienna Philharmonic above all, and the Austrian public owe him so many unforgettable musical experiences that today I can only thank him in a few words, until we hold our formal commemorative services in Vienna. We thank him and we pray that the Lord will reward him in a better world for the precious beauty he has given us in his art.

PABLO CASALS

Memorial Broadcast, RIAS Berlin, December 7, 1954

THE unexpected news of Wilhelm Furtwängler's death was a painful shock for me. Furtwängler was one of the most admirable artists I have ever known, an artist divinely favored.

Of faultless taste in the interpretation of the great masters, he made his music live with all its brilliance, all its power, and all its radiance.

My admiration for Furtwängler caused me to reply to his detractors on several occasions, and to defend him from the biased criticism directed at him. Though in conflict with "traditions" and sclerotic "schools", the Master who has just died was a faithful servant of the immortal spirit of music. I am deeply sorry to hear of his death, and I bow humbly before the mortal remains of this eminent artist.

VICTOR DE SABATA

Memorial Broadcast, RIAS Berlin, December 7, 1954

W ITH deep emotion I turn my thoughts to the great artist Wilhelm Furtwängler, who has passed from us so prematurely. His name has been linked with Milan and La Scala for many years, as an important part of our musical life. He was deeply bound to all those who truly love music, and his memory is so inspiring that it lessens our grief at his death. Through the miracle of modern recordings, his personality and the testimony of his art remain with us. I am sure that I express the feelings of all his Italian admirers: in this hour we feel ourselves closer than ever to the rest of the world, when we say that Furtwängler will never be forgotten.

EDWIN FISCHER

Memorial Broadcast, RIAS Berlin, December 7, 1954

W E honor a great man, the musician Wilhelm Furtwängler. We honor him in sorrow and respect, yet we shall remember him not only here and now but forever: for in all those who heard him, a part of him lives on, as in him a part of the spirit of Beethoven lived on, a precious gift of divine origin. He was a German musician, not in the narrow sense—for his culture, already influenced in his youth by the Greeks, was much too broad— but in the Faustian sense, that of eternal struggler and seeker. His outward appearance was that of a noble man, a figure from Gothic sculpture, as seen in his resemblance to the statue of the Knight in the Bamberg Cathedral. So also within him: the restless, impulsive, ever dissatisfied, self-torturing character was his Faustian side. He was rarely content, and shook at the gates of heaven and hell. How often he changed, edited, and improved his compositions!—And with this, we come to the center of his life, and his tragedy: composition.

Furtwängler, who wished to be considered not as a conductor who composed but as a composer who conducted, met difficulties from the very beginning, in the unfortunate première of his *Te Deum*, and only in his last years was it acknowledged that he had something meaningful to say as a composer. Performances and publication of his symphony followed, and his *Piano Concerto* was received with great esteem and success during a tour of the Berlin Philharmonic Orchestra. Generally speaking, however, Furt- wängler shared the fate of all great symphonic composers, namely the arduous conquest of the difficulties confronting great works

37

lasting more than an hour, especially when the scores are not yet published. It is particularly tragic in his case because he courageously upheld all the good material in modern music, and the list of such works he performed, including many premières, is a roll of honor for him. There no really productive name is missing, and his intervention for Paul Hindemith at a critical time honors him even as the first German performances of *Le Sacre du Printemps*. But what we carry with us, which can never be lost, is his exemplary interpretation of the great works of musical literature, from the *Passions* of Bach to the *Ring* of Wagner.

When we ask ourselves *what* the essential aspect of his interpretation was—and is, as we still perceive it in his recorded performances—it is the sincerity of his feeling, the sense of form, the law of inner progression and harmonious agreement of contrasts. This sense of the homogeneity of the individual sections, the sense of the great inner line, the sense of identification with the composer, were his alone and are his legacy to us. He was a rare master of orchestral colors, able to guide them to an illuminating yet mysterious life: at the piano too he possessed colors of an unusual, very personal charm.

In order to give clear expression to his ideas he often took up the pen, and his newest book, *Ton und Wort*, gives us a visible testimonial of the broadness of his spirit, of his untiring work on the great problems of music. After his performances, when he conversed with the composer or soloist, he revealed his knowledge and familiarity with all literature in a way that may well be termed phenomenal: and what a marvelous experience it was when he sat down at the piano and himself showed how he heard the work within him! He was of the opinion that it was impossible for the composer to write everything he wished into the score. There is, then, a "second power" necessary, which we call "interpretation". Further requisite, however, is a spirit related to the creator of the work—and there lived in Furtwängler this kindred spark of divine fire for the greatest of the creators, Beethoven, Brahms, Bruckner, and Wagner.

One thing he leaves behind in addition to his works: the enormous, educating, humane influence which he exerted upon all those who came into contact with him since the beginning of his career. How he conveyed his spirit to all his orchestras, how his experience influenced the younger musicians and stamped his seal upon them, whether they be the great old orchestras, the Vienna and Berlin Philharmonics, or a younger one, as the London Philharmonia! How I know from my own experience what peace his grandeur emanated, as his sure and beautiful hand led the excitement of his soloist back to the clear path of the composition and forced him into the service of the work—as he himself during his whole life knew only one task, to be a loving and humble servant in the great temple of immortal Art.

YEHUDI MENUHIN

Memorial Broadcast, RIAS Berlin, December 7, 1954

FURTWÄNGLER was perhaps the last exponent of a tradition carrying us as far back as the Indians and the Greeks, a tradition of music as a hallowed link with divinity, with the Gods. As we all too tritely say, nothing is sacred today, but I believe something should be and some music should be. Furtwängler accomplished a sacred rite each time he conducted a Beethoven or a Brahms or a Bach work.

Furtwängler had to be met, understood and appreciated on his own ground. He explained himself badly. In fact he was the last of an age that did not expect a man to be both creator and salesman at the same time. In listening to his music it is the impression of vast pulsating space which is most overwhelming. Compared with this infinity so many other conceptions seem willful, arbitrary, narrow and repetitive. For Furtwängler music was a world, a cosmos, which encompassed all others. He was really complete and himself only when immersed in this ethereal medium of pure energy and pure light. He almost suffocated when submersed within the day-to-day world, as would we if we were plunged into the ocean.

As human beings we are said to have evolved the water medium into that of land and air. Retaining the aqueous environment for all our inner functions, I maintain there is a further sphere, a third, beyond water and air: call it cosmic space, the realm of pure life and energy which a few human beings have penetrated. This is Furtwängler's realm wherein he was prince and priest. He seemed to hold astronomical space in bond, and brought a vision of prophetic majesty wherein all trace of profane compulsion was absent. His music was sacred and obeyed an inspired compulsion beyond anything arbitrary or man-made. No commonplace motives, expedient or otherwise, could be found anywhere remotely associated with his music-making.

More than any other he could make a Beethoven or a Brahms symphony live and breathe, expand and even address us as if with words; as it were, tearing off yet another cloak of the many we wear to hide ourselves from ourselves. We stand naked and revealed before Beethoven and judged. No wonder we sometimes almost prefer a more superficial and perfunctory performance. No intellectual, but rather an inspired mystic in the mediaeval German tradition, a man with almost infallible instincts and with the certainty and assurance of one who has seen visions and followed them.

We must find in ourselves the devotion and the conviction necessary to carry on to future generations the mystic tradition he embodied, the age-old concept of music as the link between man and God. We must find inspiration in his memory, for our ears and eyes can still recall the grandeur, dignity and intensity of Furtwängler on his podium and in the recordings he has left. In our harassed world we are not likely to find similar inspiration again so quickly. I am grateful to fate, that enabled me to share his last years. I am heartbroken that he was not spared a few months more so that he could bring his message to a grateful United States, which was waiting eager and impatient to accord him the Triumph he deserved. My heartfelt and deepest sympathy goes out to a Germany, whose highest expression he was and of whom the German people could be justifiably prouder than of almost any other exponent.

LEOPOLD STOKOWSKI

Memorial Broadcast, RIAS Berlin, December 7, 1954

In Furtwängler German art and the whole musical world have lost a tremendous artist. His style was unique. No one can ever replace him.

BRUNO WALTER

Memorial Broadcast, RIAS Berlin, December 7, 1954

THE death of Wilhelm Furtwängler signifies a bitter loss for the world of music. His spiritual home lay in the sphere of the great Classical masterpieces, and the combination of deep artistry with his unusually kind personality made him one of the most influential figures in the musical life of our time. I remember well my impressions of the very promising, high-minded young man of about twenty-one, whom I met as a rising apprentice conductor at the Strasbourg Opera, at that time under the direction of Hans Pfitzner. And I know enough of his extraordinary development to testify that the Master fulfilled in the richest measure what the apprentice foreshadowed. Without a doubt there was greatness in Wilhelm Furtwängler, a greatness which enabled him to give expression to the Great in music: and I have no doubt that his achievement, so filled with deepest devotion to music, has a significant place in musical history.

ARTHUR HONEGGER

I was profoundly touched by the death of Wilhelm Furtwängler. It is a grave loss for our musical life, for this great artist has been an absolute Master for many long years. He was the true leader who could rule in the various realms of music: one day he showed himself the man of the *Götterdämmerung*, the next day he communicated to the orchestra the most subtle nuances of Debussy's *Nuages*.

The man who wrote a score as rich as his *Second Symphony* cannot be discussed. He is of the race of great musicians, and his death is a severe loss for the art of music.

December 1954

RICHARD WOLFF

First Violinist, Berlin Philharmonic Orchestra, 1903–1950

Wilhelm Furtwängler was born on January 25, 1886, as son of
the Archaeologist Adolf Furtwängler. He spent his childhood in
Munich, where he received his musical education with Max von
Schillings and Josef Rheinberger. His career in conducting opera
brought him from Zürich to Strasbourg, from Lübeck to Mannheim; soon he was famous also as a symphonic conductor in
Frankfurt, Vienna, and in the Berlin State Opera Concerts. When
Arthur Nikisch died, Furtwängler assumed direction of the concerts in the Leipzig Gewandhaus and the great "Philharmonic
Concerts" of the Berlin Philharmonic Orchestra. Furtwängler was
an orchestral conductor of extraordinary gifts: as Hans von
Bülow appeared a *non plus ultra* in spirit and intellect, a philosopher, so was Arthur Nikisch unrivalled in finest instinct for the
most beautiful tonal color. But Furtwängler possessed both these
qualities. With his overpowering personality the Berlin Philharmonic attained undreamt-of heights, indeed the rank of one
of the first orchestras of the world. A new star had risen in the
musical heavens; the Philharmonic was spurred on to its highest
achievements and enjoyed triumphs not only in Berlin but in all
of Germany and abroad. The "Philharmonic Concerts" under
Furtwängler were always the highlights of the season in Berlin.

Like Bülow and Nikisch before him, Furtwängler was not only
the great master conductor, he was also the best friend of the
Orchestra, and helped settle all financial and political difficulties
it had to face. He was our great benefactor. In the Nazi era, what
lengths he went to in trying to save our Jewish members, our

45

half-Jewish members, and the partners of mixed marriages! In spite of all his desperate efforts, he did not succeed in keeping the Jewish members, but he did succeed in making it possible for the others to remain in the Orchestra. My wife was Jewish. When my son wanted to marry, Furtwängler ran from pillar to post to obtain the official consent necessary. "Dear Wolff", he said to me, "your son belongs to us too!".

Furtwängler could have enjoyed a secure and comfortable life abroad during the dreadful years of the Nazi régime, but he felt it his responsibility to stay behind and help educate the younger German generation, and to keep alive some spiritual values in Germany in her darkest hour. One can hardly believe now what he used to say openly against the Hitler régime; every sentence could have cost him his life. We of his Orchestra are still deeply grateful that he stood by us.

When I saw my dear Master and chief for the last time, four years after my retirement, he was especially kind and friendly to me. "You certainly look well, Wolff", he said to me. "I must retire soon myself!" "Yes, Doctor", I answered, "you have just conducted twenty-two concerts. What are you going to do to-morrow?" "Tomorrow? I'm conducting in Vienna." "So *that's* your retirement, Doctor!" I answered, and we both laughed. Now I can speak no more to the great Master. I am infinitely indebted to him for all the beauty he has given me with his music through so many years. His memory will remain with me and all the members of the Philharmonic, cherished forever.

Berlin, December 1954

SIR THOMAS BEECHAM

Remarks at the Royal Philharmonic Memorial Concert
in Royal Festival Hall, London, January 18, 1955

I shall not speak to you tonight about Wilhelm Furtwängler's musicianship. You know enough about that. He was a fine musician and a man of the highest integrity. In the difficult times in Germany he protected the weak and assisted the helpless. My tribute is to a man of remarkable and sterling character, and we see very few of them anywhere in these days.

GEOFFREY SHARP

Furtwängler: An Appreciation

from the Program of the Royal Philharmonic Memorial Concerts
led by Sir Thomas Beecham in Royal Festival Hall, London,
January 18 and 20, 1955*

WILHELM Furtwängler died of pneumonia at Baden-Baden on the thirtieth of November, 1954, at the age of sixty-eight. There can never be another; a fact fully appreciated in Germany where he trained the pre-war Berlin Philharmonic to a pitch of excellence unknown to the modern generation, and also in Austria, where in recent years he had automatically become a bulwark of artistic integrity against the progressive commercialization of the Salzburg Festivals. Newspaper articles, many of them of doubtful provenance, have made it clear that the English care for none of these things; but that this discredits the English rather than Furtwängler is evidently a subtlety which these scribblers lack the wit to recognize. Details of his life may be found in books of reference and also in Berta Geissmar's *The Baton and the Jackboot*. But his life as such was less remarkable than his work which this article must make some attempt to summarize.

At least part of the secret of the truly fabulous impact which the finest of Furtwängler's interpretations made on every genuinely musical listener lay in the deep sense of dedication to his art which permeated his performances and inspired him to superhuman feats of purely musical communication. For him music was essentially a spiritual experience; he maintained that music was a power for good—almost a moral force in itself—and he believed what he said. Of course this high moral tone would have been of little use unleavened by the gusts of genius which so

* This article appeared, in substantially the same form, in *The Music Review*, XVI/1, February 1955.

frequently replenished and intensified Furtwängler's musical imagination, itself an ever-glowing fire. Here often was a seeming spontaneity—e.g., in Marcellina's *aria*—an individual approach which, however long studied and refined, almost always appeared freshly inspired and to have been coined anew.

Furtwängler had mannerisms in plenty; the occasional obdurate rhythmical "puffings" like a model steam locomotive getting under way; the intense, almost fanatical vertical shaking of the head; and, in calmer moments, the curious practice of hanging his left hand out to dry—almost as if it were no longer a part of him. But these were not subject to variation; they remained outward and visible signs which, on familiarity, one ceased to notice; while the content of all the music which interested him remained for him a treasure-house of human experience which he illuminated in varying perspectives according to his lights, which could be very searching.

Concert-goers will remember the preliminary "stabs"—as if at some predatory insect—with which Furtwängler used to preface the start of Beethoven's most famous symphony. But they will most probably not remember their number, for professional players have been known to admit uncertainty as to which was the operative beat; yet as a rule the illusion of precision was complete and absolute. It has been suggested that this apparent unanimity of rhythm, which was such a feature of Furtwängler's performances, was achieved—in a sense paradoxically—through the very flexibility of what I have called the water diviner's waggle: the stick being held very loosely, yet impelled to a wavering delineation of rapid notes of short duration. This personal technique may be paraphrased as control without regimentation; while its barely credible efficacy at the hands of its inventor was proved time and again over the years, especially perhaps in the famous passage in the *Leonore III*, where it has long been an English tradition to skip half the notes. Furtwängler articulated them all.

As interpreter, he excelled in Wagner, Bruckner, Pfitzner, and the large-scale works of Beethoven and Brahms; while the fundamental Romanticism of Gluck, Weber, Schumann, and Richard Strauss could always be relied upon to strike a provocative and rewarding affinity with Furtwängler's volatile and responsive nature. If his Mozart was more often portentous than especially perceptive, his Haydn was bucolic, downright and utterly unsophisticated. Exceptionally, the writer remembers a beautifully conceived and balanced interpretation of Vaughan Williams' *Tallis Fantasia* and also a superb demonstration of how to play the solo harpsichord part of the *Fifth Brandenburg Concerto* on a modern grand piano without disrupting the intrinsic style of the work. He was indeed a versatile musician whose instinct usually steered him clear of those composers and works for which he would have proved an unpersuasive advocate. But even the great have skeletons in their cupboards, though the *Second Daphnis and Chloë Suite* and Bartók's *Concerto for Orchestra* were the only pair of Furtwängler's of which the writer had personal experience.

If his average level of achievement was on a higher plane than most of his colleagues ever attained, the pinnacles to which his genius could occasionally soar were quite simply beyond the scope of any others and will probably remain so. One such was a performance of Beethoven's *Choral Symphony* in Queen's Hall in the late thirties (which Geissmar regarded as his greatest single achievement); another was Bruckner's *Eighth Symphony* in Salzburg in 1949. Subsequent history lends support to the writer's contention that these two closely related works assumed for Furtwängler a very special and indelible significance. Later performances of the Beethoven—at the Albert Hall in 1948 (with very inferior forces) and again at Bayreuth in 1954—showed that he could, apparently at will, distil the essence of a composer's outpourings and present it without dross, adulteration or embellishment. A respected colleague's description of Furtwängler's last performance of the Bruckner in Vienna shortly before he died equally reinforces that unforgettable experience of August 1949.

It is primarily as an outstanding interpreter of the music of others that Furtwängler will be remembered and revered for many decades to come. He was also a competent composer with two symphonies and a piano concerto among his principal works. His thematic material is often original and occasionally distinguished, but the compositional procedures are too obviously derived from the various great composers whose interests he served so brilliantly throughout his career.

OSKAR KOKOSCHKA

When one must believe those who have seen the gravedigger performing his duty for the mortal remains of this ingenious artist, then one thinks too of those who can never realize what their loss was, because they have never seen the artist himself. Furtwängler was an ambassador from another world, a world holding him firmly in its power, and he broke free from it only because he had a message to impart. Our world has lost in him perhaps the last who could never understand, to the end of his life, the affectations of the "fashionable": in the style of anarchy and momentary successes at any price, as the art of our time expresses it. I think especially of Germany, where no personal representative of the Government attended his funeral. Yet it is to him above all, who sacrificed his life for Art and not Art for the present moment, that thanks should be given if in Germany in a time of spiritual aberration many a man remained conscious of a world of the spirit, a world based on an existence constant in a more inner vision and not dependent on customs of the time, ideologies, and terror.

And now it has come to pass that a world of such endless horizons as that of Beethoven's symphonies in Furtwängler's interpretations, has been extinguished with his mortal body, where it had found its physical form. Then one asks oneself, what caused the death of Wilhelm Furtwängler, if not this very Self which alone could save this inner world? Or is it not so, that he was preparing himself for the last journey so clearly and so surely that we all would have considered it impertinent to try to restrain him? We could only try to console him through this present age. In vain too had friends begged Socrates to turn his back on the ungrateful city of his birth and live elsewhere! One cannot, however, live in another age, and so Wilhelm Furtwängler, ever friendly, looked toward his voyage to the world of shadows as if to his only liberation.

A rare man, undeviating in this age of ours, when character threatens to become so uncommon!

One says, " Man must live!"—but there is no obligation to do so. The supplications of nearest kin, the art of physicians are of no avail where the will to live is missing. Could he have thought so? Do not clergymen already preach to the congregation, not to listen to the church-bells any longer but to hearken to the sirens of the temple of technology, for there beats the pulse of the future?

Even in his obituaries, this German was reproached for not seeking security abroad while the spiritual plague raged in his German fatherland. Misunderstood he remained too in his undeviating struggle with the obscurantists who "no longer find in art the language of their destiny", to whom "art deeply felt has become unnecessary". The obscurantists today place opposite a "classical" art of the past, somewhat as the historian isolates it from the living organism of music, a "modern" art which pleases the fashions of the day. Furtwängler was obliged to fear that he would not remain victor in his struggle, he who as no other artist suffered because his opponents consciously or unconsciously prepared themselves to overpower that realm which is of God and not of Caesar.

It is hard for the writer to send his last greeting to the friend he revered. To the guest whose visit in our house a few days before he left for the sanatorium where he was to die, did not lead us to suspect that there would never be another meeting.

I was the last to imagine as possible the fatal results of this sudden illness. Fortune willed it so that I, delighted with the youthful manner of his gait as he so leisurely came to us through the meadow, noticed only how good he looked. Each of his hands was a beautifully moulded organism in itself; and those large, clear, radiant eyes under the mighty brow! I still cannot believe that the coffin, and not the laurel branch, awaited him.

He was a seer. As he stood before my painting *Thermopylae* and began to speak—really to think out loud, clearly and precisely, yet as if no longer from this world—I suddenly thought that I understood a mysterious message from my guest and friend. He had seen with me the development of this painting from beginning to fulfillment. As surprised as if by a vision, I can only say that before all, one lonely man looked across from the world of the spirit.

Contemporaries have nothing in common with this world of the spirit; they have run aground in their vague and facile concepts of "art of our time". And as it was given to the chosen few in the age of barbarism, to read what had been written, so was it given to him, the poet of sound Wilhelm Furtwängler, to penetrate to the heart of things. He was a true sage. I regret having betrayed too much. For one should remember what Furtwängler said of the sage, that the sage could say as little about Beethoven as the Christian about faith.

Villeneuve, January 28, 1955

PAUL HINDEMITH

Address accepting the Pour le mérite Award of the German Government
in Bonn, June 18, 1955

W E have become accustomed to seeing periods of musical history symbolized in persons, in musicians. We consider them as the typical representatives of their art and their age, though they are just as much driven on by the course of history as they helped drive history onwards. We still think of the early Burgundian and Dutch musicians more as the co-ordinate parts of a great course of development, in spite of their familiar names and wonderful music rescued from oblivion. Later, however, the profile of individual musicians wins its place: Palestrina impressed the stamp of his being on nearly a century, and only by degrees did people grant places of equal honor to his contemporaries Gabrieli and Lassus. To us, Monteverdi has become the main figure of one of the most important phases of musical development; Bach and Händel were this from the beginning, though it was precisely Bach who appeared to his contemporaries somewhat as an outmoded conservative. In the age of Vienna Classicism too, it is still the composers who appear to us as the personification of all musical endeavors of their time. Only in the nineteenth century did this point of view change and broaden in one respect: the virtuosi now joined the composers in sharing musical renown. Next to Schumann, Wagner, Verdi and Brahms, the virtuosi Paganini and Liszt succeeded in winning considerable fame: and it is also in that age that for the first time a conductor —Hans von Bülow—achieved world recognition. We ourselves have witnessed the last part of this development, wherein all kinds of musicians, not only the creative ones, share in fame and honors.

If after some decades we were to look back upon the musical life of the years between the two World Wars, especially music which by and large followed traditional paths, there would be hardly one composer who might strike us as the typical musician of the age. On one hand, the public was all too inclined to evaluate musical life by events on the concert podia and operatic stages: thus the composer, working at his desk far from the scene where his music was performed, was clearly overshadowed by the performing artists. On the other hand, a development in technique and style of composition had obviously reached its conclusion: Reger and Debussy were already dead, and the important works of Strauss and Pfitzner had already been written. What now has form and value in musical composition had not yet been completed and so had not gained recognition. Composition had become self-expression without restraint, technical acrobatics or bombastic showpieces; composers worked with means which do not seem odd to us today but at that time were certainly not easy to grasp.

Yet there remained among all musicians one man who had already proved his worth very early—indeed, immediately after the First World War—who survived the destruction of all Art in Germany, and who rose again after the Second World War as the representative figure of German music, perhaps of his entire generation: Wilhelm Furtwängler.

What made him greater than all other musicians was certainly not only his musicianship—there have been many gifted conductors since the time of Bülow, and in the art of music-making perhaps no one was to be compared with the unforgettable Nikisch. What was especially original in our friend was the immense purity with which he conducted, a purity such as Bruckner possessed. His critics and enviers themselves knew well that the instant he raised his baton, the soul of the music alone stood before us—through him, its medium, this soul itself in its most convincing form spoke even to those who had envisioned some other tempo, movement of phrases and structural development. We all know the "possessed" musicians who take all obstacles by storm; we know the overpowering technicians of the keyboard, the voice, the strings and the podium; we have heard the "mystics" who know how to serve up every trace of harmony from the Tonic to the Dominant as "heavenly revelations"; we know the eternally restless who make music only "to leave no second of their existence unfulfilled", and we know the expedient career-makers. He was none of these.

Furtwängler possessed the great secret of proportion. As he understood how to interpret phrases, themes, sections, movements, entire symphonies and programs as artistic unities, so was his entire existence as a musician governed by this sense of proportion. I met him early, in 1919, and when he warned me in friendly conversations not to allow myself to fall into composing experiments (or what he then considered as such), I immediately felt his sense for the proportions of compositions and their application in performance. Later this often acted for my benefit, even when I was sometimes inclined to see as the practical point of view of a conductor what in reality was serious concern for the development of music. This same concern, this very same sense of proportion made him struggle for the just treatment of oppressed musicians during the Hitler years, at a time, indeed, when everyone foresaw the hopelessness of such struggles and he himself was in danger, playing as he was the role of a Don Quixote. This same sense of proportion it must have been that made him throw himself into the arms of the conductor's profession—which outwardly brings success again and again yet often strives for merely momentary effects—instead of dedicating himself entirely to the more penetrating and enduring profession of the composer; this same sense that finally drove him back to the podium though he was already seriously impeded by illness and weakness.

In an age such as ours, which has almost lost the sense of meaningful proportion in creative and re-creative music that he showed in a most genuine and beautiful way, Furtwängler has proved himself as a strong dike. Not like the guardians of tradition, so often dead in their own lifetimes, who always interpret new ideas as degeneration, but with a musicianship combining the most practical, substantial knowledge and the rarest idealism, he was actually strong enough to stem the tide of ruin.

The music of our time is moving from tradition to anarchy. All values have fallen into fluctuation, sensation alone seems to be the highest of all goals. Quiet study and ripening development no longer exist for the composer, as little as culture and self-assurance among the listeners. Compositions, virtuosi, styles of performance, convictions—all this changes more quickly than the fashion of hats. As the very latest fashion, even the view that "it cannot go on this way" seems to be gaining ground. Perhaps today even a man with Furtwängler's purity could no more halt the general breakdown than he could accomplish against the art-destroying madness of the Nazis. But we recall how at that time his courageous persistence gave new hope to all those in despair, and how his example was more effective than all the unleashed madness of those in power—and outlasted it, because of his righteousness. Furtwängler became the standard after which all music consciously or unconsciously patterned itself, a standard which is missing today and which, if we still possessed it, would spare us detours and eccentricities. We have seen that the pure sense for the well-proportioned is stronger than other motivating forces in music; we have seen the magician who achieved this move among us and we have loved him.

This gives us the right to say, "We miss you. We have lost your power of understanding, of moulding, of offering us beauty, and in the midst of abundance, we have remained alone, impoverished". Impoverished too, for we saw only how this man was great in his profession—indeed, unrivalled—and we failed to notice that this profession hung about him almost accidentally, as a coat. What drove Furtwängler onward was more. It was a deep belief in the fundamental truth of the Beautiful, a belief which enabled him to understand how to transform musical experiences into confessions of faith: and whoever can do that is more than a conductor, more than a composer, and more than a pianist. He is simply a truly great musician and a great man. In this form of his being, he was closely related to the mediaeval masters, who always practiced their art *ad maiorem Dei gloriam*, and in this sense his image will live on in us, to make music for us in the future, as a *scientia bene modulandi* again and again to be created, perceived, and experienced.

BERNHARD PAUMGARTNER

Memorial Address given in the Salzburg Festspielhaus, August 17, 1955

It is one of music's mysterious characteristics that its great works in their true essence are much less changeable and destructible than all the creations of the plastic arts, be they of marble or bronze: and equally, that all musical creations need a second, interpreting Master in order to appear before each new generation as a living thing, not a museum-piece, and to remain entirely effective in their ever-changing tones. In addition to what has been created in a particular, culturally conditioned period of time yet still endures, ingeniously exerting its influence over later generations, there is the power of the interpreter himself, which grows ever stronger in each new age and constantly draws energy from new inspirations. From so many thousands who attempt to be such an artist without ever surmounting the superfluities and imperfections in their skill, from a thousand other mediocrities in whose hands the ideal appears with but pale lustre, there comes before us very rarely—and only in astral hours—a *real* Master: one in whom we all joyfully recognize what cannot be taught or even described, the marks of quality possessed only by the truly great and ingenious interpreter. For only in his spirit does the imperishable arise to that second, vibrating life, only in his hands do greater mysteries than we could ever imagine ring out: we sense the thrill which overpowers us in the presence of the work given fulfillment. Deeply stirred, each time we discover anew the joyous, ringing confirmation of the eternal power of a godlike ideal in the sacrificial fire of its new awakening; and while past spiritual expression and present action seem to unite and glow in a true *unio mystica*, we experience the sound and word of the music as clearly as in the breath of its own composer. As we listen, we forget time and place and the years which separate us from the day the work was written. Here lie the important mission and the blessing of the interpreting artist. He must be a true priest, a *pontifex* or bridge-builder, a Master filled with godlike spirit who bridges the gap between yesterday and today, between the *res facta* of the work and the ever-changing mystery of its performance.

What a tremendous task is placed before the man called to rule the most magnificent yet most subtle instrument of our realm of sound: the orchestra! Here where the leader commands not only orchestral choirs but individuals and souls as well, the personal, communicating power of the interpreter assumes gigantic proportions. It has grown steadily, ever since the concept of a *maestro di capella* has existed: from the exquisite gestures of ancient choral practice, from the strictly-defined raising and lowering of the arm in the epoch of the time-beaters, from the music scroll which beat firmly against the leader's desk in the Baroque age, from the director at the harpsichord or the first violin, from the more polished beats of the baton in the late Classical and Romantic epochs, to the magnificent, technically, agogically and psychologically ever more refined modern art of conducting. Stimulated by Richard Wagner more than any other figure, this art has made its steep way upwards with the aid of many brilliant musical personalities. The names of these men will always remain in the history of music, even if some of them did not leave behind creative works of permanent value: Hans von Bülow, Hans Richter, Felix Mottl, Arthur Nikisch, Karl Muck, Gustav Mahler, Richard Strauss, Felix von Weingartner, Franz Schalk, Clemens Krauss, Bruno Walter, and Arturo Toscanini. Salzburg is proud that it has won almost all these Masters as helpful friends and active standard-bearers of its cultural goals and achievements.

One of this splendid, golden group bestowed on us by Mozart has vanished from us, before we could possibly imagine his earthly task fulfilled. His name shines more brightly now, among the unforgettable: Wilhelm Furtwängler.

Like the best of these, he became our friend, yet more: our adviser, our helper, our mighty musical champion in a critical period, when the Salzburg Festivals were attempting to rise to new achievements and new brilliance after the upheavals of a frightful war. Even before the war we had succeeded in making an alliance with him; in 1937 he conducted the Beethoven *Ninth* here, in 1938 *Die Meistersinger* and one concert. But in 1945 we stood once more at the bitter beginning. We did not have much more than our dear city, badly bombed; the old Domplatz, the Festspielhaus; the awareness of a richly justified tradition, and the memory of how it had been. Fate was kind to us when we found Wilhelm Furtwängler. With his friendly genius and great artistry, with the weight of his personality—a real *primus inter non semper pares!*—he assumed the difficult task of founder and artistic director, at first hesitantly, then confidently and with passionate devotion.

In 1947, as we were still engaged in the slow consolidation of our Festivals, Furtwängler took over the leadership of orchestral concerts and continued to carry it on in the following seasons. This was his first bold step on our side, at a time when we had to fight again for world recognition amidst newly flourishing competition among festivals. In 1949, he conducted a now historic performance of *The Magic Flute* in the Felsenreitschule — a production which became especially famous and remained on the program in the following years—and in 1950, *Don Giovanni* and *Fidelio* in the Festspielhaus, all landmarks of a new and promising rise; in 1951, in addition to orchestral concerts, a fiery and unforgettable *Otello*. In 1952, sudden illness kept him from the Festivals, but in 1953 he led a production of *Don Giovanni* in the Felsenreitschule and *Figaro* in the Festspielhaus; in 1954, already overshadowed by death, he conducted *Der Freischütz* and the same *Don Giovanni*. On August 30, 1954, Furtwängler conducted a Beethoven concert with the *Seventh* and *Eighth Symphonies* and the *Grosse Fugue*. It was the last time the Master raised his baton in our Festspielhaus, the last unforgettable impression of his noble figure before our Philharmonic.

In addition to such artistic triumphs, which have always been the highlights of our Festivals, we must not fail to assess Furtwängler's achievement as our spiritual guide, coach, adviser and friend in the last years of his rich and active life. When we asked something of him, he was always ready to help us with his knowledge, his experience, his youthful enthusiasm, and the power of convincing which his incorruptible artistry furnished him. Occasionally it did not appear easy to clear up difficulties with him; so much the nicer was it, then, to reach an understanding with him on a high level. Misunderstandings never lasted long; they often resolved themselves, and we gratefully learned to value his rare individuality.

His premature death was an irreparable loss for us and for our Festivals. It will remain so, even when the wound must heal in the course of time. It will one day be the task of the historian to establish objectively this irreparable loss. It is our consolation that he belonged to us. It is also our pride before history. And his spirit lives on in our thoughts and our plans.

Many valuable books, countless essays and evaluations of Furtwängler have been written, and quite rightly so. These recount important facts about his life, his career, his successes and his struggles, his inimitable personality, and his own important

63

creative achievements. But let us remember him in the personal magic of his tall, thin figure; in the grand dimensions of his artistic passion; in the breadth of his talents and understanding; in his noble gestures when he led his orchestra and singers; in the absolute truth of his interpretations, even if they sometimes appeared to deviate a little from the commonplace rules of the day. For as an artist he was always right. It was something divine that spoke through him, an inspiration which we should continue to share as a light and a blessing not to be lost, in this, by no means best of worlds.

FRITZ SEDLAK

Concertmaster, the Vienna Philharmonic Orchestra

THE year 1954 brought the Vienna Philharmonic Orchestra hard strokes of fate: as the sudden death of the unforgettable Clemens Krauss had meant for us and the world of music the loss of a most striking personality, so the death of our beloved Wilhelm Furtwängler dealt us an almost mortal wound. Yet the death of Furtwängler did not come to us as a surprise, for we had been worried about him since his first physical collapse in 1952, and we were forced to see — in spite of our hopes for improvement — that his health since that time was very unstable. As he mounted the podium one would never suspect this, of course; charged with energy and tension, he still knew well how to lead us in performances wherein we often surpassed ourselves.

Furtwängler was a musician who always conducted with the heart, and therefore always stirred our hearts. We played the Beethoven *Ninth* on four nights in succession in 1951, in order to meet the great demand, and the fourth performance was fully as magnificent as the first: Furtwängler knew how to draw his listeners and his musicians into his power again and again. Once, during a tour, when for technical reasons we were obliged to play a Bruckner symphony eight times in succession, we marvelled how he prevented any relaxation of our energies by his enormous intensity and inner concentration in each performance. It was one of his great gifts that he could always bring to his listeners often-played works as if they were being heard for the first time; and he often assured us that it was the hardest task of all to perform a work which we had both played countless times — for instance,

Schubert's *Unfinished*—as though it had freshly flowed from the composer's pen.

Furtwängler's rehearsals were extremely stimulating for us members of the Orchestra. He did not content himself with restricting us to the exact regard for the dynamics, but was especially interested in the essential mood of a work, in what stood "behind the notes". For this he always found the perfect expression: when he spoke of the "tearless grief" in the slow movement of the *Eroica* each of us knew exactly what he meant.

We liked to call Furtwängler the Master of Form, because he so masterfully understood how to build and work intuitively toward the climax of a score. A particularly impressive example of this was his ingenious construction of the Passacaglia in Brahms's *Fourth Symphony*, which from beginning to end showed an unbroken, irresistible forward motion. As hardly any other conductor he was a master of transitions, and worked with us— and with himself—again and again to unite tempo changes within a movement with the smoothness that prevented the dissolution of the movement's structure through exaggerated *ritardandi* and *accelerandi*. "Smooth" was an especially favorite word of his during rehearsals. It was because of his art of handling transitions that he was so unusually successful with Bruckner symphonies: he could weld often problematic finales into a unified whole, even though their sections sometimes appeared to be placed next to each other like squared stones.

As uncompromising as Furtwängler was in artistic affairs, he showed himself equally conciliatory in personal matters. Each of us he treated with friendliness and kindness, and he knew how to clothe an occasional rebuke in a form which never wounded. He was conscious of his own artistic worth yet always esteemed the artistry of his co-workers. Generally he was of a serene disposition, in jests often as naïve as a child, and he never vaunted his own superior position. When he was occasionally subject to nervous tensions—as such artists are—he rushed from the podium rather than allow them to explode, and he was very easy to soothe again, if one remained calm with him. I know this from my own experience as executive of the Vienna Philharmonic in 1945–1946, when it was necessary to master many a situation delicate for both sides.

We lose with Furtwängler a friend whose deep and warm kindness toward the Vienna Philharmonic proved itself when times were hardest. To be sure, this was sometimes made difficult for him because his own country—understandably enough—would have been very glad to claim him for itself alone. In 1930, our alliance with him had become so restricted that in two seasons he appeared before us only twice, on the occasion of the Nicolai Concerts, since the Berlin Philharmonic would have lost its municipal subsidy if he had not been willing to direct most of his activity to Berlin. Furtwängler did so with a heavy heart: but fortunately for us this interruption did not last too long. I believe it was at this time that he made his already noted remark in his *gemütlich* South German accent, "Yes, I'm married to the Berliners, but you Viennese are my darling sweetheart and I can't break away from you!"

And in fact he could not break away from us. As our country fell under the Nazi dictatorship in 1938, there soon lay on our desk the order of dissolution of the Vienna Philharmonic. As a result of Furtwängler's energetic intervention, this order was withdrawn. He also succeeded in keeping members of the Orchestra whose wives did not meet the requirements of prevailing racial laws. In 1945, such facts were unfortunately ignored abroad, and many people attempted to discredit Furtwängler on political grounds; this grieved him deeply and forced us to lose his services for two years.

His loss for us cannot be calculated, and we who were privileged to work with him for three decades are now alone. But he has left in our hearts an enduring monument. And if the words of the poet be valid—that the dead have really died only if they are forgotten by the living—then Wilhelm Furtwängler remains for us immortal.

EMIL PREETORIUS

On the morning of December 1, 1954, as the newspapers with the familiar, impressive picture of Wilhelm Furtwängler announced to the world the painful news of his unexpected death, some of us recalled the verses of Hofmannsthal

> He went out suddenly, like a light.
> We all bore, as if from lightning,
> The reflection of pallor in our face.

At that time there was no one who was not overcome by the fear that this loss had a special meaning: with Furtwängler something unique had passed from us, whether one chose to think of him as musical creator, interpreter, or simply as a spiritual phenomenon. And the anxious question followed, whether our frantic, self-doubting, rapidly self-negating existence, entangled in a ceaseless mechanism, would still be capable of creating and sustaining a personality of his greatness, a man of his unlimited gifts, passionate devotion, and artistic strength nourished from the heart.

It is now more than twenty-seven years since I made Furtwängler's acquaintance as we prepared a production of *Lohengrin* in the Berlin Municipal Opera which blazed the way to a stylistically uniform, wholly new realization of this Wagnerian work. Later I was scenic designer for him many times in Berlin and Bayreuth, in Salzburg and Milan. And I remember vividly with what élan, with what exactness and concentration he dedicated himself to the preparation of a work; how he let nothing escape his attention, above all how he saw to it that the music gave final direction to the action on stage. He never interfered with my creative sphere; he seemed to trust that I with my work materials, figures and colors, would not contradict the meaning and essence of the music. But occasionally there were very excited and fundamental disagreements over stage direction, by no means easy to resolve.

Besides the works of Beethoven, Gluck and Mozart, it was Wagner's music-dramas in particular that led Furtwängler to engage me as scenic designer. He felt himself especially indebted to Wagner, indeed in his artistic being and feeling most deeply related to him. Furtwängler's admiration for the great magician knew no bounds, and it grew with the objections and critical assertions which were made against Wagner's essence and achievement. Only with this in mind is it possible to understand a remark he made in a letter to me from Rome at the end of 1953: "I have just conducted the entire *Ring* on the radio, and I have again realized that this work is one of the very greatest feats a man has ever accomplished. Even as oratorio, this work has no equal." In a later conversation, he gave a special and surprising meaning to these words in this explanation: as soon as one detaches Wagner from all stage-action, then for the first time is it possible to grasp wholly the significance, the individuality and wealth of ideas in his musical creations—though this might contradict Wagner's basic ideal of the music-drama, as Furtwängler had to admit. He referred to the new production of *Tannhäuser* which he had just heard in Bayreuth, whose outstanding musical achievement he could fully appreciate only by closing his eyes.

I saw him again in late Summer 1954 in Salzburg, where he had conducted *Der Freischütz*. He spoke of his decision to renounce opera entirely, and emphasized his belief that the greater the music of an operatic work is, the less it achieves just and full appreciation when it remains linked with the all too diverse and distracting stage set. And he hastily added that he meant above all Richard Wagner, as strange as that might sound at first. He had therefore planned to limit all Wagnerian works to purely concert performances in the coming years; he was convinced that this would present a new, quite surprising and truly marvelous impression of Wagner as musical genius, an impression which would shame and silence every doubter and every critic.

But I need not speak of Furtwängler the musician here; greater writers will do that. I should rather speak of the man, the friend, and of the beautiful, rich, heart-warming memories of many hours through many years spent at his side. That joint production of *Lohengrin*, indeed that very first day which held us in conversation until nightfall, laid the foundations of an intense, fruitful, and confidential friendship, a friendship never clouded or exhausted until its all too premature end.

Furtwängler's interests were very broad, his view turned to the most diverse spiritual spheres, and there was nothing in the problems of modern life that was unworthy of his meditation and clarification. Our conversations, which were by no means limited to the arts, were lively and frank; they moved in many directions, in seriousness, jest and irony. After we had greeted each other with the customary questions and answers, we at once energetically attacked the problems to be discussed each time. The scene of such conversations was more often than not an unusual one, since the restless, active Furtwängler, ever on his travels, had to fight for and save opportunities to see me; and as far as my own work allowed, I was always ready to go to him. Every day, at any hour, telephone calls, telegrams, special delivery letters or other messages could reach me, nearly always in the accents of greatest urgency and impatience, demanding an immediate appointment. So we met at the airport, in the waiting rooms, often late at night; in dining cars and hotel rooms, before, during, and after his concerts. There are not too many European centers where we did not meet and enjoy our spirited conversations.

At these meetings, my partner in conversation showed an astonishingly extensive reading, encompassing even the most recent books of importance. One could explain his wide reading, the product of ceaseless effort, only by pointing to his natural and ever-alert feeling for worth as his guide in the abundance of new literature. And one other thing was enormously impressive, namely the firmness—so rare nowadays—to say *yes* or *no*, to be permitted to say it, to be obliged to say it because of inwardly felt values. As unresolved, as flexible, as easily influenced as Furtwängler could sometimes be in other respects, when it was a question of human or general problems which he considered important and which demanded a clear statement of position, he showed that he was a man entirely at peace with himself, a man who achieved the power of compelling persuasion by this indestructible unity. We often discussed topics at considerable length, but failed to reach final conclusions then and there, so we later resolved them in detailed and thoughtful correspondence. It was always difficult to defend oneself from the weight of his arguments, from the clarity and basic principles of his reflections. Far from any literary or intellectual dialectic, they had something naïvely elementary, something of an unspoiled power of scent which allowed me to detect a grain of truth even in his most daring assertions.

There were many well-known stories—not without reason—about Furtwängler's great sensitivity and easily aroused bitterness toward reviews wherever, whenever, and however criticisms were expressed against him, even when the nature and origin of such remarks were without the slightest importance. Friends sometimes had a difficult time restraining him from detailed and angry retaliations, justifications, counterattacks, even insults, before the public. Yet in spite of such hypersensitive reactions, Furtwängler was nothing less than a star in the usual meaning of the word, with the corresponding mannerisms. His world-wide fame, which surrounded him everywhere and caused admirers to follow after him and crowd around him whenever they caught sight of his tall figure and striking head, he bore with sovereign indifference; but it could become burdensome to him if it entailed the pressures of social formalities. For his entire way of life, his habits and favorite pastimes were simple, easy-going, and of an almost childlike carelessness and love of life. This was especially noticeable if one was outside in the fresh air with him, or if one wandered about with him, went swimming, sat on the lawn, gazed at the clouds or looked at plants or animals or any number of such things. One cannot possibly imagine a more candid, cheerful, unassuming and dependable comrade.

The manifold questions and doubts raised by this age—this vacillating twilight hour in history, this hour of transition from old to new—aroused more than any others Furtwängler's feeling of responsibility, his meditation and passionate interest. Thus the subject of our last conversation and correspondence was a lecture planned for the late Autumn of 1954 as part of an important conference at the Bavarian Academy of Arts, of which Furt-wängler was a member. We had conferred in great detail about this conference many times in advance. The order of speakers was to begin with Martin Buber, who was to introduce the central ideas of the symposium. He chose to develop the subject *Man and his Culture*. Then the three arts gathered in the Academy were to be represented by Oskar Kokoschka, Thomas Mann, and Furtwängler as great exponents of nearly a half-century of artistic development.

Furtwängler was not entirely clear about his lecture and said at one point that there were really two interlocking themes to be treated. One, the settlement of the basic question of existence, whose solution was that Art as a biological function must take into consideration the creative nature of man if it is itself to survive; with the increasingly technical world all around us, we must bear in mind our nature as human beings. Allowing the modern technical world to dictate what kind of Art we should produce, or to prevent us from producing any more at all, meant only one thing: surrender. The inclination of many in this direction he termed an intellectual and particularly German disease. He added that only the ever-growing knowledge of man, as it had been ideally set forth by Goethe, could save us.

As the second theme, he tried to explain the present situation, which he believed arose out of the pressure, in a rationalized, technical age, to keep open the entrance to chaos, indeed to lead the chaotic directly into Art and the creation of Art. In this way the possibility of achieving organic form, valid symbols, and meaningful artistic production for society was being obstructed. The two themes were closely related; it was merely a question whether the treatment of both was possible in a single lecture.

Furtwängler's main ideas, outlined here, corresponded to a statement he had made earlier, on the occasion of a lecture of mine concerning Goethe. It always seemed to him that Goethe's decision to place man in the center of all considerations and let this suffice—that is, to discover nature in man and through him—has not yet been understood in all its implications. He felt that we were obsessed by a so-called scientific view of nature which detracts from man, and because of this, we were neither just to nature nor to ourselves. What people so tritely call piety, which in one way or another has marked the history of the world from its origin until now, was becoming fundamentally impossible because of this attitude. He maintained that this is also the reason for contemporary artistic impotence, the unspeakable suffering and terrible absence of freedom in our whole life. He was convinced that Goethe's passionate turning toward a humanly recognizable world was founded on a presentiment of the disasters which even now fall upon us. In this sense Goethe was much more alive for him than Heidegger, Jaspers, or any other modern philosopher.

He remarked several times that this planned lecture would not sound pleasant to many ears: it expressed ideas which most people would hesitate to express, since an artist cuts off the branch on which he sits, as it were, when he utters such truths. Yet it had become bitterly necessary to spell them out as distinctly as possible in order to counteract the threatening and increasing derangement in the sphere of artistic being and creativity. For him it was above all a question of calling for reflection: reflection, this should be our motto in this hour of frenzied and ever more mechanical existence. He had not made up his mind about the title of his lecture: *The Irrational in Music*, or *Chaos and Form*, or simply *Remarks of a Musician*. When he had finished writing the work, the title still had not been decided.

He wrote to me joyfully when he had finished, but because of all kinds of unfortunate complications the letter was very slow in reaching me. Thus, worried over my silence, which he had not expected, he wrote the following lines. As they stirred me then, so will they always move me deeply. They are his last words to me, written barely two weeks before his death.

Dear Friend:

You do not answer me at all, so that I must almost assume that you feel offended. I must beg you not to do this. At the moment I am not at all well; I have had a fever for some days now and simply could not have been in Munich on the nineteenth, the date planned for my lecture. I only hope that I can be at my post in December.

With many sincere greetings,
your Wilhelm Furtwängler

He has left his post. An incomparable, pioneering, outstanding conductor, one of the chosen few who wear the countenance of creators, has passed from the world, and the world has lost in him a figure of destiny in the true sense of the word. His towering body—lithe, as if possessed—his emphatically broad gestures, the enchanting power of his passionate, singing heart, in liberating and strengthening have affirmed again and again the indestructible validity of great Art through darkness, chaos, and outrage.

III

LOUIS P. LOCHNER

On December 5, 1941, the city of Vienna tendered a banquet in its famous Hofburg, for centuries the residence of the Hapsburg dynasty, to the invited guests who had attended, during the preceding nine or ten days, the Mozart Festival honoring the one hundred and fiftieth anniversary of the great composer's death. A few hours previously, we had listened with reverent attention to Mozart's *Requiem*, conducted by Wilhelm Furtwängler. Nobody who heard his inspired reading will ever forget the scene: the famed Vienna Philharmonic Orchestra at its superb best; the vocal soloists rising to rare heights of beauty of tone, technical perfection, and moving interpretation; Meister Furtwängler conducting ecstatically, as if in a trance; the audience refraining from the usual enraptured applause at the end and instead continuing to sit as if in silent prayer, until a prominent citizen slowly rose from his seat and walked toward an exit as a signal that it was now proper to leave.

I had gone to Vienna from Berlin to report the Festival for The Associated Press. Mingling among the hundreds of guests before we took our seats at the festive board, I soon found myself near Furtwängler. After a hearty greeting, he motioned to me to withdraw with him into a corner of the huge reception hall. The reason was obvious: he knew that Nazi informers were all around us.

"Oh, this terrible war", gushed forth from his lips as though they had been forcibly held back until restraint was no longer possible. "Why did we ever get into it? Tell me, what's going on in the musical world outside Germany? You cannot imagine how isolated I feel. I don't know what my colleagues elsewhere are doing. I have no access to the works of contemporary composers in other lands. Our German cultural heritage is truly great, but we hold no monopoly on excellent music. It's most depressing not to know what is going on in the rest of the musical world."

Only once after that did I see Furtwängler again—eleven years later, after Germany's cataclysmic defeat, when I found myself in Germany collecting material for a book on German industry and its relationship to Adolf Hitler's dictatorship. The Berlin Philharmonic Orchestra, to whose annual series of concerts under Furtwängler's baton my wife and I had subscribed throughout my quarter century of service as American correspondent assigned to Germany, was on tour. We were spending some months in Essen, the heart of industrial Germany. With their beloved conductor once again in command, the *Philharmoniker* treated the Esseners to an evening of unalloyed pleasure.

And yet—it was not the same Furtwängler. His speech, as I talked to him in the Green Room, was halting. He looked emaciated and ill. He seemed utterly exhausted after an evening's conducting—quite changed from the Furtwängler of my Berlin days, when he seemed buoyant and elated after a successful performance.

Obviously his nerve-racking quarrels with the Nazi authorities, the constant danger to his life for his persistence in trying to keep Art separated from politics, his humiliating trial in a Denazification court for alleged espousal of Hitlerism (from which he emerged triumphant), his disappointment at finding anti-German sentiment in the United States still so strong that his contracts to conduct the Chicago Symphony in 1949 and to give a series of Berlin Philharmonic concerts in this country in 1951 had to be cancelled—all this had so undermined his health that he died

November 30, 1954, of pneumonia, only a few months before he was at last to have taken his Berlin musicians to America for a nationwide tour.

One may question the wisdom of Furtwängler's decision to continue to serve his chosen art under National Socialism. But nobody can question his courage under most difficult conditions. Let me illustrate this point by a few examples: Nazi protocol demanded that every conductor, on facing his audience, must raise his hand in the Hitler salute when any officials were present. As far as I know, and certainly during the many concerts which I attended, Furtwängler never did. He could have been arrested because of this violation.

Not content with omitting the obligatory salute during ordinary concerts, he even made only his customary bow at a performance which Hitler and several in his entourage attended. This could well have been interpreted as a case of *lèse majesté*. He should have turned ostentatiously to the section of the Philharmonic Hall where the "Führer" and his party were seated and given him the salute. I was present on this occasion and can testify to this courageous act. Friends told me that Furtwängler similarly omitted the salute during the Bayreuth Wagner and Salzburg Mozart Festivals.

A second series of courageous acts stems from his defense of and care for the Jewish members of the Berlin Philharmonic Orchestra. The Nazis were particularly angered at the fact that the First Concertmaster, Simon Goldberg, was a Jew. His dismissal was demanded. Furtwängler refused. In a talk with me at the time he said: "Goldberg is one of the best concertmasters in the world. I spent weeks and weeks giving auditions to applicants for the position. Nobody among that able group measured up to young, nineteen-year-old Simon Goldberg. He has fulfilled my every expectation. Why should I now dismiss him?"

A dramatic climax to his insistence came in the Spring of 1933, when a benefit concert for the Mannheim Orchestra, of which Furtwängler had at one time been the regular conductor, was to be given jointly by the Berlin and Mannheim orchestras. The concertmaster of the Mannheim musicians, who could never have made the grade for this position with his Berlin colleagues, proudly displayed his swastika and demanded, as did the management of the Mannheim ensemble, that he play first violin during the benefit event. Furtwängler adamantly refused. He had already rejected an earlier request by the Mannheim management, communicated to him at Berlin, that no Jewish players come to Mannheim. Furtwängler further compounded his "crimes" against Nazism by staying, not in a hotel, but at the home of his secretary's mother, who was a Jewess; and by refusing to attend the banquet which followed the joint concert, because the Executive Committee of the Mannheim orchestra had come to him after the concert to accuse him of "lack of national sentiment".

The unequal fight ended when, sometime later, Furtwängler learned that Goldberg was to be arrested. Again he showed courage in arranging for his concertmaster's departure from Germany, just as he did for his Jewish secretary, Berta Geissmar, when a concentration camp threatened her, and as he continued to do for one after the other of the rest of the Jewish members of his orchestra.

During that first year of the Nazi régime, some of the foreign correspondents who were Jewish were still in Germany; soon they had to leave. Among them was my trusted friend Gershon Swet, now an accredited Israeli correspondent at the United Nations Headquarters in New York. During his Berlin assignment he represented Polish and Russian noncommunist dailies. Like myself, Swet is extremely fond of music; in fact, besides

this fact could shame the Nazis into permitting Art to continue for Art's sake unaffected by political change. His colleagues abroad differed equally passionately with this point of view. But at no time did they accuse him of favoring any part of Nazi ideology. The most vociferous of his dissenters was the late Bronislaw Huberman, one of the greatest violinists of his time. His letter of refusal to come to Germany under Nazism, addressed to Furtwängler, was dated Vienna, August 31, 1933; his Open Letter to the German Intellectuals was published on March 7, 1936, in *The Manchester Guardian*. Both deserve careful study. They are to be found in *Two Worlds of Music** by Berta Geissmar, for many years Furtwängler's and later Sir Thomas Beecham's private secretary.

Furtwängler's decision to become active again despite the humiliations to which he had been subjected was expressed to me in these terms, as closely as I remember and can reconstruct them from my diary notes: In troubled times like those conjured up by the violent Nazi régime, decent people look for a spiritual escape, he argued. There is nothing as efficacious as music to transport a suffering soul into a realm of solace, repose, and temporary oblivion of the ugly facts of daily life. Yes, even tough, apparently unsentimental men of action cannot escape being softened when exposed to immortal music. His fellow-countrymen, he said, knew where he stood. His bending before the wind, as it were, and accepting insults from the Nazis, would never be interpreted by his friends and followers as evidence of his sympathy for or capitulation to the Nazis. On the contrary, they would feel that he was remaining faithful to them.

No less a person than Fritz Kreisler agreed with him. In paging through my notes accumulated while writing the biography of

* New York, Creative Age Press, 1946

this great violinist and composer, I came across the following note dated November 20, 1951: "Fritz asked that in the German edition he be permitted to add a special tribute to Furtwängler who, he testified, had behaved 'fantastically', and who, he said, had advanced artistic creativity 'in a colossal manner'. He added that he was 'enraptured at Furtwängler's nobility of attitude and pride of spirit'. Whenever Fritz mentions Furtwängler, his eyes light up as he recalls the wonderful musical treats which he owes this conductor."

My personal opinion, for what little it may be worth, and with the advantage of hindsight behind it, is that the harm done by Furtwängler's return from his Bavarian exile to the Nazi-controlled podium, and the interpretation to which this act lent itself even among many of his friends, probably outweighed the solace he could and did bring to aggrieved souls. I must support his contention, however, that to many Germans Furtwängler's music offered the best form of escapism from the realities of Nazified daily life. This was true especially after Hitler had declared war upon civilization.

During the two years of Hitler's attempt to conquer Europe and before his declaration of hostilities against the United States, my wife and I chanced to hold season tickets for the Berlin Philharmonic concerts in a box so far forward that we were virtually in a line with the conductor and hence could look into the faces of hundreds of listeners on the main floor of the *Philharmonie*. Many tough, stern-looking Nazis in uniform now occupied the seats in which many of our friends had sat in happier times. In other seats we saw many a worried, anguished face awaiting Furtwängler's raising of the baton. An undeniable transformation took place after but a few moments of music: furrowed, worried brows straightened out and became relaxed; often a beatific smile played upon the lips; the stern, unsentimental, frozen expression on the faces of the men in uniform, a good percentage of whom were on furlough from the front, was gradually changed at least into satisfied detachment and even positive friendliness. Music doth indeed have charms to soothe the savage breast!

I believe one may well think of Wilhelm Furtwängler and his behavior under a régime which ran contrary to all that he held dear, much as the free world thinks of Boris Pasternak, who also tried to live in accordance with his own faith and beliefs, but who was humiliated and insulted again and again by a dictatorial communist régime which should have been proud of him.

HUGO KOLBERG

Concertmaster, the Berlin Philharmonic Orchestra, 1935–39 and 1958–63

I⊤ is both a pleasure and an obligation for me to write something about Wilhelm Furtwängler and to recall my personal impressions gathered during my years of work with him. I not only had the honor of being his First Concertmaster in the Berlin Philharmonic Orchestra for four years, but I was also given the privilege of introducing his *First Violin Sonata*, on five evenings in 1937, with himself as accompanist. This gave me an opportunity to be in close personal contact with him for months and to understand and enjoy his greatness as a musician.

Before I assumed my post in the Berlin Philharmonic, I had been First Concertmaster of the Frankfurt Opera House and Museum Society Orchestras, and had been able to experience all the great moments of Frankfurt musical life: unforgettable opera and concert performances under Karl Muck, Richard Strauss, Clemens Krauss, Otto Klemperer, Felix Weingartner, Bruno Walter, and many other world-renowned conductors. In the years following my emigration on racial grounds from Nazi Germany to the United States, I enjoyed further opportunities to play under famous conductors, including, of course, Toscanini. He was one of the most ingenious conductors, and in his interpretations of Italian operatic music, quite incomparable. His interpretations of German Classical and Romantic music, however, were far behind the spiritual grandeur which Furtwängler discovered in interpreting this music: no other musician possessed the power of expressing the "inner law" of this music with such vital force as Furtwängler.

Concerning the question of Furtwängler's political attitude

and with Furtwängler's defeat, that moment seemed to have come. The Executive Committee of the Berlin Philharmonic asked me to go and see Furtwängler, in order to persuade him to resume his role as our protector against the Nazi authorities — at least to go to England with us. Furtwängler was very surprised to see me as mediator; I had to admit shamefacedly that I had acted utterly without thinking. Furtwängler was very worried about the future of the Orchestra, but he remained steadfast in his decision. He added that he wanted to get away to Egypt, to fulfill an old dream, and that he intended to devote his time to composing. Things turned out differently. The next day the government "requested" him not to leave the country. After several months' pressure, Furtwängler at last had to agree to a compromise, to return to concert life without official posts. The feeling that he had deserted his Orchestra was a very important factor in winning his agreement.

In the summer of 1935, I gave up all hope that the Nazi régime was just a passing thing. I came back from my vacation in Austria with the firm intention of resigning from the Orchestra. Furtwängler would hear none of this, and he tried to convince me to stay on. His argument was that the Nazi régime would collapse in six weeks. After the war it became known that a group of generals had planned a *Putsch*, and, since Furtwängler was close to resistance circles, it is entirely possible that he knew of this. In any case, I carried out my decision and left Berlin on Christmas 1935, to take a post in Ankara.

In the summer of 1937, I met Furtwängler again, when he visited me at Zell am See in Austria. We spent three days together and had a good long talk. I tried to persuade him to leave Germany, but he would not listen. He was terribly depressed and answered that Germany was the only place where he could be of use to Nazi victims. "It would be so easy, not to come home after one of my tours abroad. But that would not help anyone in Germany." As is well known now, he intervened for many Jews and other persons who were politically "undesirable" to the Nazis, to such an extent that he was warned by the government. Indeed, I learned from a member of the Swiss Embassy in Ankara in early 1945 that the Swiss Government had given orders to all border posts to let Furtwängler into the country, whether he tried to cross the frontier by train, automobile, on foot, or even on skis.

I hope that these observations will help correct the erroneous political image attributed to Furtwängler in the past.

HEINZ UNGER

Wᴵᴸᴴᴱᴸᴹ Furtwängler was at the helm of the Berlin Philharmonic Orchestra during the years when I developed from a
musical fledgling into an orchestral conductor. The inspiration I
received from his performances, and the personal encouragement
he gave me in conversations in the beautiful Sonnemann home
on the Matthaeikirchstrasse in Berlin, were not forgotten by me
during the dark years which separated me from Germany, and
they never will be forgotten.

Our personal contact was not restored until 1954. It was in
a warm and cordial correspondence which we both hoped
would be a prelude for a personal meeting, either in Toronto,
where I had made my home, during the first North American
tour of the Berlin Philharmonic, or in Berlin, where I was to
give my first postwar guest concert, under Furtwängler's invitation.

His death intervened, and I was never able to ask him personally
how he had been able to survive the dark age in Germany without
suffering severe damage to his soul. It was obvious to me that
political interference in matters of Art, as everything else that
happened in the Nazi era, must have been abhorrent to him, and
the numerous cases of his intervention for victims of the system
proved where he stood. But why, why had this man to whom
the whole world would have been open, not left the Germany
of Hitler, as so many other artists and scientists of pure "Aryan"
origin had done? This was the question which so many of his
friends in other countries asked themselves.

Shortly after the war I received an indirect answer. It was in Barcelona where I happened to meet a conductor from Germany whom I had not seen since my own emigration, Franz von Hoesslin, a former Bayreuth conductor, later living in voluntary exile in Switzerland. I had known von Hoesslin in the old Berlin days, and we had a long and intimate conversation on that day in Barcelona. Our thoughts turned to Furtwängler. Why had he not left Germany? Hoesslin told me of his own conversations with Furtwängler on this subject. Yes, Furtwängler knew that he was likely to be welcomed everywhere in the world, if he should decide to turn his back on Germany, that he would probably be successful and celebrated wherever he went. But—would he be understood? Understood in the way he *wanted* to be understood? All his roots were in German music; leaving Germany would set him adrift. Not that he would not continue to serve that art to which he was most closely and most naturally bound; but would *his* way of playing music go to the hearts of his listeners in the same way as it did in Germany? Who outside Central Europe would realize or appreciate the difference between the message of Beethoven's *Ninth Symphony* as he felt it and—let us say— Toscanini's Beethoven? No, he needed his German audiences and orchestral players as much as they needed him, more than ever, in fact, in those dark years; and so he stayed within the community into which he had been born.

Was he right? A futile and wholly unanswerable question when we face the deep conviction of a great artist who always must remain a law unto himself.

KARLA HOECKER

I~ 1943 and 1944, urban dwellers in Germany, harassed by bombings through a hundred nights of horror, had somehow managed to preserve an astonishingly unshaken feeling for all that was real and alive in Art. It was a consoling and uplifting power in those last months before the end of the war that gave music its verification, to a degree which not even the most fanatical music-lover could have foretold. The moral law in the midst of destruction was upheld by music alone: music became the echoing lament for all the tortured, defiled, and slaughtered in this age.

But who gave shape to this lament, who came again and again to barren, demolished Berlin, in spite of the constant air-raid alarms, the bombed-out travel routes, and countless other troublesome and dangerous obstacles? In the small group of musicians which can be named here was Wilhelm Furtwängler. In a time of agony and oppression his concerts were true places of refuge for all the suffering and the tormented, for all despairing and inwardly emigrated hearts. His last concerts, given under the most difficult conditions, surrounded by death and annihilation, were a triumph of the spirit over matter, our last protection.

We have no right to pass over these things in silence. Especially since Furtwängler did not have to remain in Germany. He received no advantages by doing so. The world stood open to him, because of his renown and the sensation caused if he had gone into exile after his intervention for Paul Hindemith. But he stayed behind out of his conviction that it was precisely in such a time of sorrow and guilt that an artist had to fight on in Germany, to defend the fire of tradition which, once extinguished, could never have been rekindled. He was suspected and tormented by the bitterly anti-intellectual government of the Third Reich, and his opposition frightened the régime all the more because it stemmed from the spirit and could not be drowned out by S.S. slogans.

By staying behind, Furtwängler gave consolation and support to thousands of the despairing who waited anxiously for the end of that fatal epoch: not heroes, to be sure, for they were not sent to concentration camps for their convictions, and they closed their mouths when they should have shrieked. But they suffered in their hearts and kept alive their longing for truth, reconciliation and the divine order of things.

HUGO STRELITZER

A$_{NY}$ contribution to this volume is a duty of honor for all those who admired this great man and are eager to see his reputation as a human being restored in the eyes of the many who have condemned him for his alleged "Nazi leanings".

Here is my story. Until the first of April, 1933, I had been teaching at the Staatliche Hochschule für Musik in Berlin as a coach of the opera school there. I was then fired without any notice for racial reasons. During the following months I directed several workers' choruses, and in August 1933, during one of our rehearsals storm troopers appeared and took me away with some Jewish-looking members of my chorus. They threw me into the infamous prison, the Columbia House, and I disappeared. Luckily for me, my sister had been present at this rehearsal, and she notified all my musician friends of my disappearance. Through a friend of an "Aryan" pupil of mine, my friends learned my whereabouts, but here ended all their endeavors to help me.

I had never been a member of any political party, and had never indulged in any political activities. The only thing that was against me was the fact that I was a Jew. My friends felt at that time there was only one man in Berlin who might help me in my predicament—and that was Wilhelm Furtwängler, who had already stood up courageously for Jewish musicians and protected them from persecution. My musician friends formed a small committee and saw Furtwängler on my behalf, explaining to him my situation, my reputation as an artist and my integrity as a man. They assured him that I had never been active in any kind of political activities, and that I was blameless in this regard.

I must emphasize here that Furtwängler did not know me personally, that he only knew of me; but he immediately gave this committee the solemn promise to intervene with the Nazi authorities on my behalf, and to try to the best of his abilities to free me. Through his secretary, Miss Geissmar, we learned much later that Furtwängler went to see the then Minister of Culture, Rust, and the then Police President in Berlin, von Levetzow, to plead my case and assure those men that I was in no way involved in any political or subversive activities, and that my reputation as an artist and a man was beyond reproach. Both officials promised Dr. Furtwängler to see that I was released in due time from the Columbia House. This conversation took place about one week after my capture. If I had to remain in the Columbia House for about six weeks, it was only because it took this long for my wounds and scars to heal, received from a brutal and merciless beating the night of my capture. At that time, the Nazis did not release any prisoner unless he looked like a halfway decent human being again.

After my release, I sent flowers to Miss Geissmar to thank her for her efforts, and I asked her if I might see Dr. Furtwängler personally to thank him for what he had done for me. Miss Geissmar answered me, emphasizing that the fact of my release was a greater satisfaction to Furtwängler than any words of mine could express, and that his heavy schedule did not permit him to see all those he had helped and whose cause he had championed.

Here ends my story. If I am alive today, I owe it to this great man whose wonderful and courageous attitude has been slandered by those who could not understand why he had stayed in Germany under the Nazi régime. But while he stayed in Germany Furtwängler helped and protected many Jewish musicians, as long as it was humanly possible to help them. I feel that this record is a unique one, and that it shows greater courage and fortitude than all the so-called "noble" broadcasts to the German people by those who sat safely here in America and preached humanity over the airways while Furtwängler *practiced it under the very eyes of the Nazis in Germany itself.* History will judge this man and his humanitarian work on behalf of the oppressed and persecuted long after the voices of his enemies have been silenced. I have no doubt that this present work will be a most constructive contribution toward this end, and I am only too glad that I am able to furnish it with another proof of the greatness of this man.

FRITZ ZWEIG

My acquaintance with Furtwängler began in 1919 at the Mannheim National Theatre, when I resumed my conducting career which had been interrupted by the First World War. Furtwängler, as General Music Director, was my chief: the highlight of our friendship was the long walks we used to take at night, and the discussions we had about many problems. In those years I had an opportunity to become acquainted with Furtwängler's comprehensive, universal culture, and his totally idealistic approach to all subjects. It is known to very few that during this period he conducted not only the masterpieces of German literature, but also Italian and French operas, even a new production of Johann Strauss's *Die Fledermaus.*

Later, when I was conducting at the Berlin State Opera, I saw him quite often. When Hitler came to power in 1933, Furtwängler shared the view of many opponents of the régime that "things would cool off". But in spite of his absolute innocence of the ways of the world, he soon saw that the Nazis were indeed serious about their plans, and the revolution in German musical life made him constantly take up the cause of the persecuted innocent. He helped very many flee the country and saved the lives of many others.

In 1934, in Paris, where he was indescribably popular, he told me about the shameful incidents occurring in German musical life, but declared that he felt it his duty to oppose the Nazis with his influence and not to abandon his post. On New Year's Day 1939, I saw him for the last time before the outbreak of the war.

It was again in Paris, and he was very depressed. We talked for hours, and I begged him to leave Germany before it was too late. I can still hear his reply: "But I cannot *live* in exile!" He was deeply moved, and there were tears in his eyes. Who dares to doubt the sincerity of this great idealist's word? Especially after he had already taken a position of bluntest opposition to the powers in the Nazi party!

After the war, he wrote me in the United States, where I had meanwhile found asylum, and at that time I did everything within my weak powers to gather voices of good will to speak out for him. In 1950, I saw him in Lucerne, where I heard him conduct for the last time—an unforgettable performance of Berlioz's *Damnation of Faust*.

I received his last letter a few weeks before his death. It was filled with details of his forthcoming American tour with the Berlin Philharmonic Orchestra. He also informed me that he was sending me a copy of his new book. The book arrived—like an envoy from the other world—two days after his death.

MARIA STADER

THE most impressive memory I have of Wilhelm Furtwängler comes from the year 1945. The most horrible of all wars had just ended, and the whole world was staggered by the Nazi atrocities which had just been exposed in all their hideous detail. Furtwängler was then living in Clarens, outlawed and branded as a Nazi. I could see at once how happy he was that someone with whom he could talk had come to see him. This great artist, who was only a musician and nothing else, who still devotedly believed in the good qualities of the race of poets and thinkers, realized that he had been misused for and by a régime with which he had, and could have had, nothing in common. What he had wanted was to hold his beloved Berlin Philharmonic together and thus save it from chaos. But in that time of hatred and horror who believed and understood this "pure fool"? He himself sensed how difficult it was for others to understand him. And so he lived in seclusion on Lake Geneva, uprooted and bewildered.

After this deeply moving conversation, he asked me if we could make a little music. When I said yes, he brought out the two *Passions* of Bach and accompanied me in all their soprano arias. I shall never forget this hour of Bach: of my many memories of the great artist, this is the most precious.

SARAH GAINHAM

I remember hearing and reading of the Denazification of Furtwängler while I was in Vienna. The first time I heard and saw
him was in Vienna, shortly after these proceedings. He was given
a warm ovation. Everyone discussed his "past", and the fact
that he had been labelled a Nazi maddened the Viennese. I recall
a friend who was a former Viennese and a Jewess trying to
explain how much more complicated these matters were than
we all supposed; I was still full of war propaganda then and
intensely provincial in the bargain. I remember her saying that
for an artist like Furtwängler the whole thing was a meaningless
formality that simply allowed him to go on with his music; and
if he *had* refused and thrown away not only the whole meaning
of his life but with it the comfort and release of all the thousands
who listened to him conduct, it would not have made the least
difference to anything, except to make the world even poorer
than it was. This humane and true argument seemed very strange
to me then; like many Anglo-American news correspondents, I
then spoke no German, but in the intervening fifteen years I
have worked pretty hard to get rid of my own nationalism
(the British are intensely nationalistic, though of course they
call it patriotism): and one of the first things that made me
ashamed of my own sweeping and uninformed judgments
was that this beautiful, highly cultured and elegant woman,
whose family had lost a large fortune through the Nazis, showed
more forbearance than myself, who had to a large extent escaped suffering.

Later, when I lived in Berlin for five years, I often heard Furtwängler conduct at the temporary home of the Philharmonic in
the Titania Palast. The first time I ever heard Beethoven's *Ninth
Symphony* apart from gramophone records, he conducted this
wonderful orchestra. The music has, and specially then had,
when the war years were fresh in everyone's memory, a symbolic
meaning for all Germans: the audience wept in silence instead
of applauding. It was one of the moments I shall never forget.
And I shall never forget the last time I heard Furtwängler, just
before his death, when he had to support himself with a special
kind of framework against which he could lean to take his weight.
He conducted Schubert's *Ninth*. It is one of my favorite symphonies and was gloriously played. The Berliners always played
wonderfully for him out of sheer love and, as I now think,
gratitude and respect for him.

MOSHE MENUHIN

Wᴵᴸʜᴇʟᴍ Furtwängler was a victim of envious and jealous rivals who had to resort to publicity, to smear, to calumny, in order to keep him out of America so it could remain their private bailiwick. He was a victim of the small fry and selfish and puny souls among concert artists, who, in order to get a bit of national publicity, joined the band wagon of the professional idealists, the professional Jews and the hired hands who irresponsibly assaulted an innocent and humane and broad-minded man, all because by association, by birth, he was a German. We Jews are very sensitive when all of us are called names because one scoundrel of a Jew may have acted immorally: yet just because the German people were captives of murderers and cannibals called Nazis, who were insane with racist nationalism, just because many of them conformed and obeyed their Führers, is there any excuse for taking an individual, decent, noble German and fouling his name, boycotting him, refusing him his rightful position in America, not once, but time after time . . . even long before the Nazis came on the scene . . . all because a clique of envious rivals arranged to bring up every accusation conceivable against the man, in order to eliminate him from New York, from Chicago, from anywhere, if they could have their way . . .

My son, aside from knowing Furtwängler for many years before Germany went insane during the Nazi captivity, investigated about him in Germany, in France, and Switzerland long before he made joint concert appearances with him. Mr. Edward Ryerson and the entire Chicago Symphony Association had thoroughly investigated everything possible about Furtwängler before they gave him a contract to come and conduct the Chicago Symphony. But when, like a pack of wolves, mass action was aroused, and the ignorant, the wicked, the neurotic, the mentally sick, the sensitive, the public, were poisoned, Furtwängler and all others realized that the air and atmosphere were so contaminated with ill-feeling and inhumanity, that it was out of the question to make music therein. Hence Furtwängler, of his own accord, chose the quiet way, and gave up his last chance to live here and do creative work . . . It was our loss, much more than his. But only a Yehudi Menuhin, who has to live first with his own conscience before he can deal with any outside considerations, gathered the courage, as on other occasions for Wilhelm Furtwängler, to take a stand in the face of the meanest and most dishonorable fighting imaginable. As he said in connection with the Furtwängler affair: "I do not recognize races, nations, but people . . . the individual . . ."

Furtwängler deserves that someone clear his name and point out, for the future, how hysteria, wire-pulling, mass poisoning through dishonest publicity, must be searched out in public issues. I well remember during the First World War when playing Bach, Beethoven, and Brahms was not allowed anywhere in the United States. When speaking German meant getting a bloody nose. The idiots, the adolescents our people were then blamed the Kaiser's deeds and German music, literature and language in the same breath: these were considered partners in crime with German submarine warfare. Furtwängler was a German, but he was as good as the best of us outside Germany. He wanted to make music, artistically and professionally. He did it as no one else in the world could make it. There were many thousands of Germans outside concentration camps who had to live and look after their professions and positions, and keep quiet or be shot to death. Furtwängler came close to being put in a concentration camp or shot, had the war lasted a little longer. People who are persecuted, above all others, should think twice before they allow themselves the luxury of persecuting the innocent or the unknown. Yet alas, Jewish concert artists shouted the loudest to eliminate Furtwängler, as the lackeys and satellites of the conductors who did not want Furtwängler in America. The truth, however, always comes out.

FRAU ARNOLD SCHOENBERG

Furtwängler, as a conductor, will live in the hearts of those who heard him but, unfortunately, will vanish with their passing. But he was more than a conductor. He lived for music and he deserves to be remembered like a Pope in the Church.

My memory goes back to an event at his house. After a rehearsal, through the duration of the dinner and until we left, the conversation was but questions in regard to how he should conduct a piece. He wanted to do it in the intention of the composer, who incidentally was Schoenberg.

And again: in Paris, 1933, he came to our hotel and offered to negotiate with the German authorities in our behalf. How different from Richard Strauss's ironic reply to Otto Klemperer, "Just the right moment to intervene for a Jew!"

Furtwängler knew that the Germans had done a terrible wrong to Schoenberg and he suffered for it as a German, and felt it his duty to interfere. Not only as a musician but also as a friend. But the most remarkable moment came when he, more desperate than Schoenberg, cried out: "What shall I do now?!" Arnold told him: "You have to stay and conduct good music." He did, and whatever trick was used to soil his name, instigating a whisper campaign and later a very loud one: *he never was a Nazi*.

So I shall erect to him a monument in my heart and forget the already forgotten Toscanini. Because Furtwängler tried to serve Art and not let Art serve him.

TRUDE FLEISCHMANN

THERE is one composition which is perhaps too great to be performed. Many dared to attempt it, but none succeeded. A parallel is the sunset; try to photograph it! Millions do, but no one can capture its greatness, its splendor, its awe. Because of this, the great composition went out of style; snobs and perhaps even music-lovers came to consider it as second-rate. Its name: the Beethoven *Ninth*. I must admit that I too had snobbishly rejected it, despite repeated hearings, until one day a great musician came, who revealed the divinity of this work. There were no more banal sections in this symphony; it was truly a reconciliation for all the world. The voices in the Finale came from heaven. The audience was in ecstasy, and I hope that Beethoven, in heaven where he is no longer deaf, heard it. This is how he must have imagined it, this way alone! I find that since Furtwängler conducted the *Ninth*, no one else should attempt it. In his interpretation he achieved something absolutely unique. And it was thus in whatever he conducted. Suddenly one understood what the composer wished.

People have criticized Furtwängler for not having left Germany when the Nazis came to power. He was a German, and an artist, somewhat naïve. In his innocence he could not imagine with what infamy and cruelty this government would rule. He was an idealist, and in his idealism he thought that he could help his people. He was mistaken, and when he realized his mistake it was too late. He was more or less a prisoner of the Germans.

I knew Furtwängler well, and photographed him many times. I last saw him in 1950, in Vienna, where I had returned from my adopted homeland for a visit. I was shocked to find him so changed. He was a broken, embittered man. He too was a victim of Hitler.

Let those of us who knew him be grateful that he lived, and that some of his performances are preserved. But recordings are only substitutes. One really had to *see* him conduct. He was totally absorbed in the music, without "pose" of any kind, of indescribable beauty. It seemed as if heaven itself had opened. We thank you, Wilhelm Furtwängler!

IV

RAFAEL KUBELIK

He who seeks through music the inner meaning of earthly life is guided by the intuition of his musical talent.

Furtwängler seemed to be filled with the inner clarity of a noble mind. His intuition led him to attain the heights of harmony.

And does not this search for harmony represent the whole significance of man's earthly journey?

Furtwängler has left a great heritage—the true man found peace through music.

Only the really great can achieve this.

CLIFFORD CURZON

F<small>URTWÄNGLER</small>! What memories this illustrious name stirs in me of my student days in the Berlin of the late twenties! It brings to mind first, of course, the many rapt, and enrapturing, performances he gave in the old Philharmonic Hall in conjunction with my own teacher, Artur Schnabel, of the great classical concertos; but perhaps my most vivid and lasting memory is of Beethoven's *Ninth Symphony* under his direction. The deep impression of the nobility of this performance remained with me through the passing years until I began to wonder, as one does, whether its magnificence had not really been the illusion of a susceptible student. Then, by chance, I heard a radio programme in which a recorded performance of the same work by Furtwängler was compared with recordings made by four of his greatest contemporaries, and to my enduring joy he still seemed to me, thirty years later, to be far and away the most inspired musician of them all. The name Furtwängler to me will always stand for that youthful musical enchantment which, as so rarely happens, cannot be dulled by time.

CLAUDIO ARRAU

As it is so frequently said of great artists, and so seldom true, Furtwängler really got to the marrow of everything he performed. He was not just great in the Classics, as has so often been said: he was great in everything he touched. For me, he was the interpreter one dreams of, the ideal interpreter who is able to become one with the music he interprets. Furtwängler was able to do this. Everything he touched he knew and understood. I think the greatest Debussy I ever heard was from him, and Beethoven and Brahms and Bruckner. The greatest Chopin accompaniment a person could ever hope for, came from him. He breathed every little rubato with me, every sigh, every ascent and descent. And what about his Schoenberg, and *Tristan* (shall we ever hear anything to match it in a hundred years?) and *Fidelio* and *Don Giovanni*! Everything his magic wand touched came alive as if re-created, I mean created, anew right there and then. One need only go back to his recording of the Schubert *Ninth* to realize again the infallible heartbeat of a true interpretation, and the magic and vision and total immersion of the true interpreter.

DIMITRI MITROPOULOS

I really feel a little embarrassed to write something about such a great person as Wilhelm Furtwängler, but all I can say is that all my life, since I was an unknown person starting my career, until the time I met him, just a year before his death, he was the artist I admired the most in my life, and I was rewarded when I was in Salzburg that last year of his life, to find out that he liked me, and gave the best of recommendations for me to take his place in Salzburg. I felt that was very encouraging, and it was really thanks to him that I became also a part of Salzburg, for what is left of my years to come.

New York, November 14, 1958

GÉZA ANDA

I⊤ is a difficult task to write about Furtwängler, in fact I ask myself whether a true appraisal is possible at all. The experience that *each* of his concerts meant simply cannot be expressed in words, perhaps precisely because he lacked all the externals which help describe a brilliant personality. His art was the art of *inner perfection*. For him mechanical precision was not the task of the conductor, but the expression of a musical problem's solution. He did not "shape" the broadest patterns, or "build" the crescendi, or "place" the accents. Everything arose from a musical First Cause, as islands arise from the sea, moved by mysterious powers. His interpretation of a piece was not speculative pedantry to effect "fidelity to the work", it *was* fidelity to the work because it grasped the inner pulse of the music. Furtwängler's artistry was the struggle of a human being to comprehend the Infinite through the heavenly language of music. He sought this to the end of his life. If anyone doubts that he found it, let him hear Furtwängler's recordings of the Schubert *Ninth* and the Schumann *Fourth*.

LORIN MAAZEL

The Russian fable tells us of the priest who had a dog, and one day the dog died and on the beast's tombstone was inscribed the tale of the priest who had a dog, and one day the dog died and on the beast's tombstone, etc.

The fable of Art tells us of society that makes of a few men (artists) the spokesmen of all, and one day an idea of the composer dies into a composition (is not the concretization of an idea a little death?) and in the performance epitaph (when music is played is it not a remembrance of something passed, through which the future is sought and the present modified?) is inscribed the tale of society that makes of a few men (artists) the spokesmen of all, and one day the idea of a composer, etc.

If we accept the circle concept of Art, then all points on the circumference (society, composer, performing artist, public, etc.) are theoretically of equal interest. In practice, however, the more focus any one point may have, the clearer the way seems to the next: through the expression of a great composer, society is illumined; the personality of an interpreter clears the way for auditor to composer and thus to the auditor himself. It follows then that all questions of the superiority of creator to re-creator and the place of each are superfluous.

The genius of a composer in no way belittles the society from which it springs. Quite the contrary, it is a praise of the society. The *divo* interpreter can show no contempt for music—his capacity to communicate renders the musical experience the more personal.

Furtwängler was a great interpreter. This simply means that he was able to light up the circumferential band that binds society to composer to performer to public. His language was the language of his contemporaries. Interpretation is just that: re-creation in contemporary terms. It follows again that tempo and "approach" are but means—and means of the moment. A tempo is simply the speed at which a musician feels that a given composition may best come alive under the immediate conditions (acoustics, temperature, capacity of the player and instrument, the "mood" of public, occasion, performer, and many more). This is the task of the performer and his joy—to re-create in relative conditions the absolute of the complete mystical experience.

I write this in connection with Furtwängler because he has been the subject of much sterile literature and many futile crises. Toscanini versus Furtwängler—"the Romantic approach", "slow tempi", "Germanic sentiment" and other such irrelevantia are the edifices of the artificial ambient of journalistic conception in which the figure of Furtwängler has been both vilified and hallowed. An artist cannot be judged so; he is not even to be judged in the concert hall. He can only exist—and Furtwängler "existed" as perhaps few other interpretive artists: in the beautiful music he made.

There are those who would look for absolutes in musical performances. Music, by its very need of re-creation, remains the truest of the arts to the society in which it is born, in that it can be constantly re-translated without the damage that translations must do.

I heard the Maestro's re-translations of Brahms's *Third*, Beethoven's *Fifth*, *Till Eulenspiegel* and the *Tannhäuser Overture* in a performance with the Berlin Philharmonic in Rome towards the end of his career. It was all that a concert should be, and the experience remains before rather than beyond description. One felt a sense of existing *with*—a sense that comes before thought and the word to express it.

MAX RUDOLF

W HEN Wilhelm Furtwängler assumed the Directorship of the symphony concerts in my home town, Frankfurt am Main, I as a young music student was fascinated by his novel and highly personal approach to the great German masterworks. He brought a new intensity and spontaneity to the interpretation of well-known scores. The concerts and rehearsals I attended, the oratorio performances in which I sang in the chorus under his leadership are unforgettable experiences. Furtwängler belonged to the small group of great interpreters of music who felt the call to serve the masters. His achievement was based on a combination of devotion and self-possessed courage to disregard tradition, furthermore on a mental attitude which placed the spiritual values reflected in music far above technical exigencies — an attitude typical of the Romantic era which we, the older generation, now see disappear, not without a certain nostalgia.

JOSEF KRIPS

I knew Wilhelm Furtwängler from the time I was nineteen to his passing. I knew intimately and admired his work with the Vienna and Berlin Philharmonic Orchestras, and his operatic performances in Vienna, Bayreuth and Salzburg. His personality was threefold: he was one of the greatest musicians of his time, he was a poet on the rostrum, and he was a great technician—if one understood what he wanted to achieve with his technique.

His knowledge of music in all fields was stupendous: there was hardly a string quartet he did not know by heart, he was a fine pianist, a wonderful accompanist for songs as well as an ideal companion in chamber music. Whatever Furtwängler conducted he ennobled: he took liberties in tempo and dynamics but what he did he felt so strongly that it sounded absolutely natural. Perhaps he did not always catch the "letter" of a great work, but certainly he caught its spirit.

You could not copy him—who could ever copy a personality? —but there was much to learn from his approach to music and from his way of conducting: his enormous devotion. He studied anew the hundredth performance of any work he conducted— he was never satisfied with himself and rarely with his orchestras. He knew that beauty of sound in an orchestra is the sum of the produced overtones (harmonics). He knew about the "eternal line" in a great piece: when he started the first bar, in his mind he was already in the last. He hated rough accents where they were not especially indicated: this caused his way of downbeat, which was difficult for musicians who did not know him. A member of the Vienna Philharmonic, once asked by a concertgoer, "When does the orchestra start on such a mysterious downbeat?", replied, "When we lose patience!" Yet his musicians always came in together, and there was "music" from beginning to end when Furtwängler was in command. His feeling for the "rests" was another point, for instance when there was a rest with a fermata after the last note in a movement of a Beethoven symphony—many times one had the impression that the music came from eternity and went back there. Finally, his ever-perfect balance of mind and heart.

He will never be forgotten, not by his orchestras, not by his audiences, not even by his colleagues: they all admired him. A pity that America knew so little of him.

RUDOLF KEMPE

I am delighted to provide a few remarks for this memorial volume, but I fear that the theme has already been fully treated by more skilful pens than mine. My own memories of Wilhelm Furtwängler are limited to a period of frequent concerts with the Leipzig Gewandhaus Orchestra, in which I played First Oboe many years ago, and to later encounters in the concert hall.

I believe that the artistry of Wilhelm Furtwängler has already achieved world renown, and that extensive commentary from me is superfluous. All my impressions are easily summarized when I say that for me personally Wilhelm Furtwängler was the most remarkable phenomenon among the conductors of the "great epoch", as it is called. Whether he met the demands of "modern" tendencies—especially as applied to the art of conducting or its present chaos—I cannot say. But I am convinced that of all the conductors of our time, no one achieved the unique combination of technical skill, intuitive power, and magnificent spiritual conception which marked his interpretations.

CARL BAMBERGER

'THE symphonic flow." Furtwängler coined this phrase in order to give a name drawn from the eternal laws of nature to that unifying force: the stream of the symphonic drama of sounds which subordinates motif, theme, melody, and rhythm, and makes them flow into a convincing totality—this concept became his creative ideal.

It was this synthesis of sound that always engaged his attention and drew him again and again to Heinrich Schenker, whose new ideas on musical law, basic line, and immanent energy of the single tone he often pondered and discussed. "Through this supporting role of penetration"—I recall Furtwängler's exact words—"through the conductor's constant permeation of the music, the truth of the masterpiece is revealed to the listener".

And it was musical truth that he conveyed. Interpretation seemed to become creation. One had the feeling that he was composing as he conducted, improvising on an instrument—the orchestra. All who played under him became masters forging masterpieces—through the tender radiance of his deep perception.

ALEXANDER KIPNIS

I met and sang with Wilhelm Furtwängler for the first time in Wiesbaden, about 1921. The opera was *Fidelio*, and we singers were all carried away by the fire, drama, and dedication of this man. On the afternoon of the day the performance was given, I saw Furtwängler walking in the fields towards Sonnenberg, a suburb of Wiesbaden; believing he was alone, he started to conduct an invisible orchestra, and I think he went through the entire opera.

I sang performances with him in many cities—Berlin, Bayreuth, London, Paris, and Leipzig, where he accompanied me on the piano in the Gewandhaus. Whether it was *The Marriage of Figaro*, *Don Giovanni*, *Der Freischütz*, or *Die Meistersinger*, it was always a Music Festival for me to sing with this man. Through all the years of our association, I never heard him talk of politics or money. His life was music alone. And he was generous with praise for other conductors, not waiting for their deaths to appreciate them publicly.

NIKOLAI GRAUDAN

I first heard Wilhelm Furtwängler conduct the Berlin Philharmonic Orchestra shortly before Arthur Nikisch's death. I was at once struck by the power, logic, and persuasiveness of the performance, as well as by the silken and extremely well balanced orchestral sound. When Nikisch died, there was no doubt in my mind that Furtwängler would be the rightful heir to his positions, which he actually became.

It was my good fortune that some years later I was engaged as First Cellist of the Berlin Philharmonic Orchestra, a post I held for nine years, and thus I had the privilege of becoming closely acquainted with Furtwängler's musical genius. Having taken part in all his concerts in Berlin and on tours, I learned to know and appreciate his endless devotion to his art, his boundless love for the works of great composers —sometimes in the middle of a rehearsal he would spontaneously exclaim, "*I* should like to have written this music!"—his profound penetration into the composition, and his unerring gift for the precise characterization of the work at hand.

His understanding did not know national boundaries. German music was, of course, his home, but his interpretation of French music evoked enthusiasm in Paris, and Russian music in his hands could not sound more Russian to my Russian ears. I particularly recall an incident when Furtwängler helped the violin soloist to find the correct character of the theme to the variations in the *Suite* of Taneiev.

Furtwängler played the piano beautifully, and he was able to play at any time any of Beethoven's sonatas, quartets, and so on.

He played on the orchestra as freely as a pianist would play on the piano. He was aware of the technical difficulties such freedom involved, and he once told me that it was no problem for an orchestra to play together as long as the conductor beat the time squarely and inflexibly; the difficulty began only when he made music freely. Furtwängler himself was sometimes criticized for his "delayed beat", but he explained the merit of this device by recalling his first rehearsal of the *Eroica* with a foreign orchestra. The opening chords sounded like the popping of a champagne bottle, he said, but the delayed entrance created a tension which resulted in a powerful explosion.

Furtwängler had an intense dislike of mechanical reproduction of music; he was too much a musician to be interested in the technical aspects of broadcasting and recording, and he only reluctantly agreed to submit to the demands of the mechanized era. Considering this, we have to deem ourselves fortunate to have recordings of a number of great compositions in Furtwängler's inimitable interpretations. But we sorely miss the choral works of Bach, Haydn, Beethoven and Brahms, in all of which Furtwängler so eminently excelled. For my part, I shall always be grateful to my fate for offering me the chance to work with and to learn from one of the greatest interpreters of great music.

SIR ADRIAN BOULT

I still have a most vivid recollection of my first hearing of Wilhelm Furtwängler in the historic Concert Hall in Vienna, in 1922. The programme consisted only of the *Ninth Symphony*, and the orchestra was the Vienna Symphony. I imagine that the opening of the *Ninth Symphony* is one of the most impressive things in Beethoven's whole output, and somehow on this occasion it seemed more exciting than I had ever heard it before. And as the First Movement developed, its eloquence and the extraordinary vividness of detail brought to my mind some apprehension as to whether the enormously rich colouring and flavouring of the opening ten minutes could ever be consummated as that amazing seventy minutes of music developed to its climax. I need have had no fears, for the whole performance emerged as a thing of perfect balance, and as we left the Hall there was no doubt that we had had a most rare artistic experience. Beethoven's masterpiece had here been realized in a way that was profoundly moving, and at the same time completely proportioned.

I am so glad that memories of Furtwängler are being collected, for the life of an interpreter is indeed short and permanent recollections are few, once his active life is over.

HERMANN SCHERCHEN

In 1923, at the age of thirty-two, I was Director of the Leipzig Concert Society Subscription Series, which the public of the Leipzig Gewandhaus Concerts had formed as a result of the difficulties of the inflation; the middle class in Leipzig was no longer able to pay the spiralling prices of the Gewandhaus Concerts. On one occasion, after we had performed the Sibelius *Fourth Symphony* in the Albert Hall there, we heard that Furtwängler had been in the audience. He had only recently resigned his Directorship of the Frankfurt Museum Concerts, where he had been successor to Mengelberg, and assumed leadership of the Berlin Philharmonic. Soon thereafter I conducted a concert of the Frankfurt Symphony Orchestra in Frankfurt am Main. After this concert, the President of the Frankfurt Museum Concerts greeted me with the words: "*You* are coming to us as Furtwängler's successor! He told us all about your concert in Leipzig!"

I met Furtwängler personally in 1939, when he came as guest to conduct the Winterthur Musikkollegium Orchestra, a group I had also led since 1923. He asked me if I could share the leadership of the Berlin Philharmonic Concerts with him. Unfortunately I could only reply, "That is as impossible for me as it would be for a fish to live on land!".

In Furtwängler as a conductor I always admired what was perhaps the most extraordinary talent of this profoundly great musician, the ability to respond to the spiritual needs of his public. I once heard this particularly in the Finale of the Beethoven *First Symphony;* after the slow introduction, begun *allegro commodo*, then constantly accelerated, to the obvious delight of many listeners, until triumphantly the real *allegro* broke in. And I should mention in conclusion an unforgettable *Pastorale* and later a *Seventh*, wherein the power of Beethoven's music, in Furt-wängler's magnificent performances, was so compelling that all awareness of the public's presence itself vanished.

HENRY HOLST

Concertmaster, Berlin Philharmonic Orchestra, 1923–1931

A rehearsal with Furtwängler was always a very exacting experience, partly because he demanded the utmost concentration from his players, and partly because his beat often lacked that "flick of decisiveness" which will help to enforce precision in an ensemble. That kind of precision he did not like at all: he wanted the precision that grew out of the Orchestra, from the players' own initiative as in chamber music. At times we had the feeling that he did not know what to do with his baton; he always used a rather small one. When something went wrong during a rehearsal, he would invariably shout, "Gentlemen, why don't you look at my beat?"—but alas, that would not always be a help! His left hand, however, was most expressive; with this he moulded phrases as a sculptor moulds soft clay. When an orchestra had become familiar with his highly individual way of conducting, he achieved interpretations of rare beauty. His feeling for building up a movement to one overwhelming climax was unique. This made his renderings of Bruckner symphonies unforgettable.

Furtwängler was a great instrumental instructor. He made each player surpass himself in artistic interpretation. As a rule it is recognized that playing in an orchestra is harmful to solo playing. I did not find this so; on the contrary, I owe much to Furtwängler with regard to phrasing.

Many conductors lay the foundation for the evening's performance during the rehearsal, often with the remark, "But tonight, gentlemen . . .". Furtwängler would not be satisfied with this. He wanted the evening's performance during the rehearsal: he could then nearly always rely on his own suggestive powers to inspire us in the evening to surpass the performance of the rehearsal. No wonder that after a three-hour rehearsal with this dynamic and hypnotic artist, the members of the Orchestra were exhausted!

Furtwängler was body and soul in the music and very sensitive to small blemishes. He would react visibly to the slightest mishap, somewhat in the same way as when a person suddenly gets a foreign body in the eye! In most cases this would be accompanied by stamping of the feet and violent hissing. This was not only upsetting to the unfortunate player, but also to the audience, which either had not noticed or would gladly have overlooked a slight mishap for all the loveliness he gave us. When this was pointed out to Furtwängler after the concert, he would reply that he was unaware of having given any sign of reproach.

Furtwängler's interpretations were highly individual, and woe to the admiring colleague who tried to copy his style and tempi! They would become boring, because only Furtwängler himself could infuse spirit into a slow tempo. The present vogue is for more mechanical precision, smarter tempi—and for this reason all we who came in contact with Furtwängler are grateful for what he gave us. We learned from him that the emotional experience of music is fathomless in its possibilities.

WILHELM KEMPFF

I saw him for the first time in 1923, in Switzerland, at Stazer See between St. Moritz and Pontresina, in the years when he was called "young Furtwängler". The first impression was overwhelming: at last a man on whose brow genius was written, whose eyes radiated true humanity!

This impression did not prove deceptive. Again and again in later meetings this wonderful and encouraging feeling returned, to be enriched each time, even when we had had an argument— and how he could argue! But he argued only about the matter at hand; the personal element was completely excluded. And so he became something like the musical conscience of Germany: this conscience always showed itself when he scented danger, danger in the sense that the musician—both the creative and re-creative musician—was betraying himself and no longer recognizing personal responsibility as the highest law.

For political reasons, some were suspicious of him—a man who dared resist the Nazis and boldly place himself as protector before his flock of proscribed citizens. This is fully documented, this is well known, yet it still seems to be too little known. As was Wilhelm Furtwängler the man, so was he in his art. There were no insurmountable conflicts; this life was a wonderful unity. It was permeated both by the Apollonian and the Dionysiac—who did not feel this? Who did not also feel that a third was present, Eros, the winged god, who raised him from the earth to the stars?

Thus when he conducted the *Ninth*, we heard more than merely a doctrinaire, "faithful" decipherment of the score: we were thrilled, we experienced anew the ecstasy of creation which had possessed Beethoven. And again we were proud to be members of the human race.

ANTONIO JANIGRO

Wilhelm Furtwängler! What memories, what impressions this name awakens in my heart! I was still quite young when I first encountered this great artist, this true Master and poet of music and Art. Very few conductors revealed to me so many secrets, so many truths in the works his baton brought to life. Death took him from us, alas, too soon. Fortunately his recordings, a rare treasure themselves, still radiate all his power of expression, all his depth, and his intimate, sincere musical message.

FERDINAND LEITNER

IF I were to write my autobiography, I should need to devote a long chapter to Wilhelm Furtwängler; here I can write only a few words. Since my earliest youth I attended his rehearsals with the Berlin Philharmonic Orchestra, and since I was sixteen I was privileged to provide the piano accompaniment at rehearsals for his concerts with the Bruno Kittel Choir. Among the frequently performed works were Bach's *Saint Matthew Passion* and *Saint John Passion*, Beethoven's *Missa Solemnis* and *Ninth Symphony*, Haydn's *Creation*, Brahms's *Requiem*, and many others. Often I had the opportunity to converse with him at length, and in some of these performances I played the harpsichord. Again and again I could study him as a great musician; but much more impressive to a young man were his deeply spiritual qualities. Without doubt, the knowledge and perception he gave me have played a great role in my own development as a conductor. If I must express myself briefly, my last words to Furtwängler would be: "thank you".

DEEMS TAYLOR

W HEN, as music critic of *The New York World*, I first heard
Wilhelm Furtwängler conduct the New York Philharmonic,
on January 11, 1925, I was so struck with the clarity and
deep musicianship of his interpretations that I wrote the following:

"No program is hackneyed in the hands of a conductor of the
first order. I think Mr. Furtwängler is just that. He is not a prima
donna, and he is not what is generally called a 'creative' conductor. He does not conduct, as George Barrere once remarked,
'right hand for the orchestra, left hand for the audience'. His
work must obviously have been done at rehearsals, for he con-
tents himself with beating time as unostentatiously as possible,
and indicating a few entrances, with no aesthetic dancing thrown
in.

He does not try to make Beethoven interesting, and he does
not give the impression of claiming the American rights to what
Wagner really meant. But he does know how to coax exquisite
playing out of a symphony orchestra, and he does play orchestral
music as the composer wrote it.

. . . There is a beautiful rightness about most of Furtwängler's
work. He not only gives you the letter of the law—the notes, the
tempi, the expression marks, the orchestral balance—but gives
you the impression that he is conveying the music in the composer's own spiritual terms; that he not only plays the passages
as the composer marked them to be played but has bothered to
search out the composer's motive in marking them thus."

After years of listening to Mr. Furtwängler conduct, I have little to add to this, except that he continually deepened my admiration of his skill.

JOSEPH SZIGETI

". . . I had to consider seriously the question whether there is any sense for me to concertize in a country that meets me with such a lack of comprehension. This question has been answered —as far as I am concerned—in a negative sense, long ago."

Lᴇsᴛ the reader of the above extract from a letter Furtwängler wrote me, jump to the conclusion that he had *us* in mind while writing this, let me hasten to add that the date is July 5, 1924, and the passage concerns a country in Europe, not America. However, perhaps this outburst of the great artist does after all have a certain relevance to us and to our attitude towards him at the time of his activity at the helm of the New York Philharmonic. Who knows whether a statement such as this does not shed some light on the reasons for his deplorably short-lived connection with our musical life, and whether it will not explain to some extent the unhappy fact that after his departure in the Spring of 1927 we were to be permanently deprived of his musical ministrations—a word I use advisedly. Granted that the emergence of the Nazi régime became an insurmountable obstacle to his return, yet how do we "explain away" his absence between 1927 and, say, 1932?

It so happens that I was Furtwängler's soloist with the New York Philharmonic at two of his last concerts on March 3 and 4, 1927. Were it not for the regrettable obliviousness to my surroundings that marked the self-centered young virtuoso I was then, I should now be able to say something more than just vague recollections of the uneasy, strained atmosphere backstage, the demonstrative ovations out front that seemed to protest against a "fait accompli". The chronicler of our musical scene can easily reconstruct the facts of the "case" from newspaper files. What I am concerned with is the conveying of the vague feeling of unhappiness, strain, and foreboding backstage . . . and the resigned, forgiving smile of the obviously hurt artist, a smile that seemed to answer the acclaim with a philosophical "too late!" . . .

I was able to contrast this farewell *Stimmung* with our concert the season before, with the New York Philharmonic at the Brooklyn Academy on February 28, 1926, when I had the privilege of playing the Brahms *Concerto* with him. Who then would have thought of what would happen only a year later?

But let me try and recapture other glimpses of the Master: the *gemütlicher Abendschoppen* . . . the leisurely after-dinner sipping of wine . . . in a Leipzig *Weinstube* in the early twenties in company with Charles Münch, then Concertmaster of the Gewandhaus, whose guest I was at his bachelor-quarters; the look of fulfillment on Furtwängler's face after the 1950 *Don Giovanni* at the Salzburg Festival, to which he had invited us from Bad Gastein; then in 1952, that new expression of philosophical detachment and a certain faraway look, after the concert in the Paris Opéra with the Berlin Philharmonic, when Pierre Fournier and I played the Brahms *Double Concerto;* at the supper in the Café de Paris, where his plate of fresh strawberries made *our* post-concert appetites seem rather gross . . .

I also like to remember that he, who sometimes has been criticized for not sufficiently championing the music of our time, did in fact assist many young musicians in obtaining a hearing. Especially impressive was the collaboration I heard him give Stravinsky in 1924, in the German premières of the *Piano Concerto* in Leipzig and Berlin. And was not Hindemith's *Philharmonic*

Concerto a clear enough tribute to him as sponsor and interpreter? The Furtwängler recording of the Bartók *Violin Concerto* with Yehudi Menuhin, too, was an eloquent gesture, coming as it did from an aging artist shortly before his death.

If these jottings seem inconsequential measured by the stature of the subject of this volume, it is perhaps because I purposely avoided a task hopeless for me—to try and convey to the reader musical moments of the supreme eloquence and unforgettable grandeur which I owe Furtwängler.

SUZANNE BLOCH

WHEN the Berlin Philharmonic Orchestra came to Paris in the Spring of 1928, many of us young students in the throes of preparing for examinations decided at the last minute to go to its concert. We arrived a bit late, and as we stole in by a back couloir we could hear the orchestra in the midst of a Händel *Concerto Grosso:* I found myself rooted to the floor, unable to move, so stirred by the eloquence of the music. After a long season of rather pedestrian orchestral concerts, this Händel struck me with such a vital and moving force, it seemed as if the orchestra were moving like a wheat field under the breath of a mighty wind.

I knew nothing about Furtwängler, and seeing his angular figure from a distance, I thought he must be a rather elderly gentleman. There was for me neither glamour nor personal magnetism, but simply the direct and fervent communication of the musical thought with no special effects or tricks. There was a freshness to this music reaching everyone, and at the end of the concert the audience was aroused to an emotional enthusiasm rarely found in Paris. I was deeply impressed by Furtwängler's extraordinary sense of musical structure which he brought out with great clarity; and since I had already planned to go to Berlin to study form the next winter, I decided to do all I could to attend his rehearsals. When I later wrote him to this effect, he graciously responded, saying that a daughter of Ernest Bloch would always be welcome. A fine friendship developed between us for which I can have only gratitude; the relationship was always kept on a high spiritual level, thus remaining intact.

Being able to hear a variety of Furtwängler's performances and rehearsals, I learned a great deal from him. Perhaps the most interesting experience was hearing him prepare my father's *Schelomo* for presentation in Hamburg. During the first reading at rehearsal in Berlin, my mother—one of the keenest musical critics I have ever known—cast doubtful glances at me and shook her head: nothing seemed to come out right, it was all dull and shapeless. But the more Furtwängler began to work, not on the details but on the big lines, adjusting proportions, banging out the architecture of the piece, *Schelomo* arose, vivid and beautifully understood. When the details were then worked out, it was a revelation. My mother was deeply impressed and told Furtwängler so, but he was not satisfied: on the train to Hamburg, solely concerned with the study of the score, he would come over for a while to chat, then exclaiming, "Ach, I must go back and study my score!" he would leave us. The performance was as if he had always known the music, and I wish my father had been able to hear it.

My impression of the man Furtwängler was that he lived solely for music, with his head in the clouds, hardly realizing where he walked. His secretary, Berta Geissmar, seemed to govern him in all matters of organization and musical politics. He himself was extremely anxious to better his craft, and in speaking of other orchestras he often expressed his admiration for such groups as the Boston and Philadelphia orchestras, praising strings or woodwind sections. There seemed to be no personal vanity in him, though he often repeated that he wished to make his orchestra the best.

He had great reverence for Karl Muck, and always stopped to pay his respects to the old and retired conductor when his own travels brought him near. He certainly did not act the part of a great "Maestro"; on the contrary! I remember lunching with him in Vienna at a modest basement vegetarian restaurant where he used to eat as a student; everyone sat around the same big table. On the way out he passed through a market and bought a large amount of oranges which he carried in a paper bag himself.

His patience and good humor with my extreme and over-definite youthful opinions amaze me now when I remember the statements I made. One day in discussing Bach, I sang the theme of a *Brandenburg Concerto*, as usual, quite rapidly. He asked quietly, "Oh, is that the tempo you take?" adding, "I don't take it so fast". He went to the piano and played the music beautifully himself, then asked me if I didn't think that should be the right tempo. . . .

One of the last times I heard him conduct was in 1929, when he performed the *Saint Matthew Passion* in Berlin. At that time he was going through all sorts of personal problems, and once after a rehearsal as he told me about them he tore a button off his jacket in despair. But in the concert, all this was set aside; he seemed to disappear behind the music. The audience forgot him, hearing only the great masses of sound, the anguish, the faith, the tragedy and serenity of the drama. And at the end, before the final chorus, we suddenly became aware of Furt-wängler, who seemed drained of life. There was a pause, and we saw him give a great sigh: the entire audience seemed to sigh with him. In later years, when monsters were unleashed and terror spread over Germany, I often thought of those sighs, wondered and still wonder. I shall never want to hear the *Saint Matthew Passion* again, but shall keep in my memory this perform-ance and those sighs that seem now a tragic premonition of what was to come.

ERNÖ BALOGH

My memories of Wilhelm Furtwängler are clear and unforgettable. He stamped his everlasting mark on the entire generation which enjoyed the great experience of being present at his performances. I was fortunate enough to know him well for many years: I first saw him in Berlin in 1919, and heard him for the last time on July 2, 1954, in Geneva. Thirty-five years had passed, and in those years I often had the pleasure of hearing him in concerts and operas, performances and rehearsals, in many cities.

I had the opportunity to compare him with the other great artists of the podium, and I witnessed performances under Safonoff, Koussevitzky, Weingartner, Richard Strauss, Karl Muck, Mengelberg, Nikisch, Walter, and Toscanini, not to mention the other titans of the *Taktstock* who are still alive and conducting — Stokowski, Monteux, Klemperer, and all the others. Each had his own shining qualities, but Furtwängler was the one who made the deepest impression of all, because his performances brought the composition and composer closest to the audience. This was not surprising, as he was a creative artist, a composer himself. Each of his performances sounded not as a re-creation but as a creation there and then: spontaneous, exciting, eruptive, touching, and deeply moving. This miracle, achieved through the spellbinding magic of his personality and his unbelievably close affiliation with the composition, was repeated again and again; and his faithful audience knew and expected that he would always perform it. This is exactly what I felt when I heard him for the last time in Geneva in 1954, when he conducted the Beethoven

Third and *Fourth Symphonies* with the Suisse Romande Orchestra, with hardly any rehearsals, with damaged health and damaged hearing, but with magnificent spirit and uplifting results.

When I heard him in Berlin in 1919, he was Director of the Mannheim Opera, successor of Bodansky, who had gone to the Metropolitan Opera. The name "Furtwängler" was hard to pronounce or remember at that time, even for Berliners, and it was completely unknown to them. To fill the hall, he engaged as soloist Edwin Fischer, who was then the most popular living pianist. Fischer was to play the Brahms *D minor Concerto*, which was the reason I went. But when I heard that young and unknown conductor Furtwängler, I was astounded. So was the audience. He conducted Bruckner's *Eighth Symphony* as I had never heard it before or since. That evening he led the Berlin Philharmonic, which I had often heard under the conductor whom Europe respected and loved as the greatest of all—Arthur Nikisch. One could not really compare Furtwängler's beat or experience with those of Nikisch at that moment, but his experience grew and matured. His beat improved, but was never outstanding or remarkable. While Toscanini's orchestras, wherever he conducted, were polished to perfection, disciplined to astonishing exactness, Furtwängler was quite unrivalled in his spontaneity, the soaring and singing of his orchestras without fear or tenseness, the joy of re-creating a great creation, the exalted yet relaxed, rare pleasure of making music. His unparalleled gift of communication was not to place himself between composer and audience but to eliminate the interpreter altogether and present the work and its composer directly to the listeners—or still better, to compose the work before our very eyes.

Furtwängler conducted the New York Philharmonic for three seasons in the twenties, sharing the podium with Toscanini, to whom the entire musical press was subservient, including the publicity department of the Philharmonic. All Furtwängler's concerts in New York had ended with great public acclaim; his farewell concert in the first season won such a long ovation that he was forced by the audience to make a speech, which to my knowledge he had never done before. When he arrived for the third season, I immediately warned him that according to my information he would not be re-engaged for the next season. Unfortunately, the information he received at the Philharmonic Office was the contrary: he was assured of his re-engagement, which for various reasons he never received in writing. This strengthened my suspicions and the correctness of my source. My last warning was just before he departed for Germany, but he was deceived again, and left this shore with assurances from the Philharmonic that his new contract would follow by mail. It never did. Almost immediately after his departure, announcement was made that he would not be re-engaged. This hurt him very much, and after such treatment at the hands of the Philharmonic, he felt that the only land he could not conquer was America.

In Europe, of course, it was different. There he was absolute monarch in the world of music, and during his lifetime more books were published about him than about any other conductor. In addition to these works several of his own books appeared: they treated music, to be sure, but were of a deeply philosophical nature, as the man himself was a deep thinker, broad in vision. I enjoyed most of our interesting conversations during our long walks through many cities and many years: Vienna, New York, Berlin, Budapest, Salzburg, St. Moritz. I shall always remember a discussion we had at St. Moritz in 1927, concerning the "continuity" of flow in music, even where rests interrupted the tones. And on that occasion I asked what he felt was the reason for the birth and flourishing of atonality everywhere after the First World War. His opinion was that this was a reaction against the enormous influence of Wagner, his "exaggerated" Romanticism and "over-sentimentality": the public wanted to turn away from Wagner, from Romanticism, and from the tonality in which music had been rooted. Yet he remarked that it was a great joy to conduct Wagner's music, even greater than to listen to it. His Wagner performances were incomparable: I shall never forget his *Rheingold* in the Vienna State Opera in 1929, a revelation such as I have never experienced in the field of opera.

Rehearsals were not his strength, because he was less interested in details than in the great line of a work and the depth it offered. This was the reason he neither asked for nor needed many rehearsals. He concentrated on the performance itself, where he used all the imagination, energies and creative powers he could get out of his musicians. Some of the critics, particularly in America, found his tempi too slow. Everyone, of course, is entitled to his own opinion. Furtwängler's reaction to this was, "Who is a more competent musician to know what are correct tempi—the critics or I?" In his younger years, his fast tempi were exceedingly fast, but as he grew older they became less furious and excited, and this distinguished him from most of his colleagues. The tremendous, rapid tempi of today, their aggressiveness and purely mechanical perfection, were always far from him: his tempi were relaxed and never rushed.

Furtwängler was mortal and human, with human weaknesses: he was often indecisive, and always tended to believe those near him. He was easily influenced by them and often convinced by the one who had the last word. But he was never impressed by wealth or importance; neither money nor position could influence him. He was a very simple man. I remember when I saw him for the last time, in Salzburg in 1954, how his dog followed him wherever he went and sat close to him, unwilling to leave his side. In an age of commercialism and publicity, he never had a manager or press agent or any professionally trained person to handle his affairs; his assistants were usually friends or clerks. Everything he achieved was the result of his art, without fanfare from the press or publicity of any sort. He loved nature, the rain, the woods, the clouds, and his daily walks in all kinds of weather. His heart was big, warm, and simple. For his friends and fellow humans he had understanding, respect, warmth, and love.

He was a great human being.

LOUIS KENTNER

Furtwängler was, to my mind, the last of a long line of great German musicians who were so essentially German that the musical universe, for them, began and ended with German music. This is both a strength and a weakness, and Furtwängler, who had the pride and humility of the great artist, exulted in his strength and tried to overcome his weakness: his Beethoven was heroic and warmly human and luminous, but when he turned to the masters of other races his approach was apt to be tentative, albeit always sincere. He was no fanatical martinet, and I have heard him discuss questions of interpretation with much lesser people; indeed, he would listen to almost anyone who cared to utter an opinion, however distasteful to him. This tolerance and patience first attracted me to him as a personality, having of course always greatly admired his musicianship.

In these days when so many musical crimes are committed in the name of "Classical objectivity", it is with nostalgia that one recalls Furtwängler, whose readings of the Classics were "subjective" in the extreme, whose technique of conducting was so entirely personal, and who gave millions of music-lovers of his time incomparably more pleasure than our machine-crazy generation can ever hope to get from its mechanically-minded practitioners.

SIR JOHN BARBIROLLI

THAT Wilhelm Furtwängler was one of the great conductors of his time, no one can deny, even those who may have differed from him in aesthetic and musical principles. I always hesitate to say *the* greatest of anything, for anything which is intrinsically great in conception, devotion and integrity can make a contribution to musical Art of untold worth. Such was the quality of greatness of Wilhelm Furtwängler.

WOLFGANG SCHNEIDERHAN

It is unnecessary to endorse the personality of Wilhelm Furt-wängler as a musician and a man. Where greatness is concerned, skepticism should not dominate; we should not even debate the issue. Instead we should rejoice in people who are so richly endowed by God. It is far more valuable to stress the happiness they give to the soul, rather than the common human failings they might share with us.

I shall mention here some important traits of Dr. Furtwängler which I could observe on countless occasions in personal and musical contact, as Concertmaster of the Vienna Philharmonic and later as his soloist. The rare, ideal fulfillment of musical feeling was his humanistic spirit. Each time his interpretations were born in elemental force, and the public was swept along by the irresistible power of his art. He led rehearsals with the same intensity as concerts. There was no modern "economy", no extreme precision as in routine recording sessions. He hated the emulation of mechanical perfection, for he knew that in the final analysis this was a false idol, unimportant when weighed against true musical values. Even when we rehearsed longer than usual, we played on, firmly within his power. Looking back on my years of association with Dr. Furtwängler, I am very grateful for the guidance and inspiration which I received from him.

RUDOLF FIRKUSNY

As I never had the opportunity either to play under or meet Wilhelm Furtwängler, my contribution can only be of a very general nature, from an admiring listener. Unforgettable indeed are the Furtwängler concerts I had the privilege to hear before the Second World War. Old masterpieces in his interpretations became new experiences: his insight, uncompromising attitude and absolute idealism combined with sacred fire, made them sound like new, almost improvisational creations of the moment. This highly personal gift of Furtwängler, together with many other qualities, made him for me one of the truly great conductors and personalities of our era. And we who heard him shall always cherish these moments of great beauty and accomplishment.

LAURITZ MELCHIOR

THE name Wilhelm Furtwängler is for anyone who experienced his outstanding musicianship and who worked under his leadership, a name never to be forgotten. I myself worked in Richard Wagner's operas with him many times around the world, and what he contributed to the performances by his treatment of the musical score will always be remembered. Of course, Wilhelm Furtwängler was first of all a symphonic conductor and because of this, he sometimes was more occupied with his men in the orchestra pit than with his singers on the stage; but after you had got used to his beat, you could be certain that you were participating in an outstanding musical event.

JEAN MARTINON

I remember one day at a rehearsal years ago. Wilhelm Furtwängler was at the conductor's desk. Entrance into the hall had
been strictly forbidden. I was then an apprentice conductor, and
I had just skilfully stolen into the back of a darkened loge in the
third balcony, in order to follow the Master's rehearsal with my
own scores. I had always so much admired his irresistible power
over the orchestra and his profound majesty over the works he
interpreted and enriched with his own spirit, a spirit so penetrating and so personal.

Everything was going well, when suddenly, after making the
same observation on a certain passage three times without obtaining appreciable results, Furtwängler exploded. He beat so vio-
lently on his desk that it fell to pieces, scattering the pages of
his score all over the floor. There was absolute silence; the
orchestra seemed frozen with fear. Just at that moment, as I
crouched in my seat and held my breath, all my scores slid out
of my lap and crashed to the floor like thunder. I was discovered
at once and speedily shown to the door—to my great despair,
for I had lost a unique occasion in my life to see at close range
the work of one of the most mysterious and enchanting batons
in the world.

ERNA BERGER

From the first moment I met Dr. Furtwängler, I was drawn to him by a deeply felt artistic bond. Later I often sang the soprano part in the Beethoven *Ninth;* when one could watch him during the first three movements of this work, one was totally in the power of his compelling personality. His face appeared transfigured, and the radiance of that divine music enveloped us all. He looked like an archangel!

But during intermission, this "archangel" became a little boy being scolded. At one concert, after I had sung the two Mozart arias "Mia speranza adorata" and "No, che non sei capace", there we stood—like two poor sinners—in the corners of the Artists' Room. Dr. Furtwängler was "advised" on conducting by his wife Zitla, and my husband tried to explain to me how I could best interpret the music! This situation struck us funny, and we often laughed about it in later years.

In 1934, Dr. Furtwängler engaged me for the Berlin State Opera, and my career as coloratura soprano really began. As "Ännchen" in *Der Freischütz* and in many other roles I was able to study and admire him as a conductor of opera. In London he once accompanied me on the piano when I sang Rosina's arias from *The Barber of Seville*, and I was prouder and happier than I can say. In 1953, Dr. Furtwängler engaged me for Zerlina in *Don Giovanni* at the Salzburg Festival. I shall never forget his kindly smile as he said to me one day after a splendid rehearsal, "*Bergerlein*, you really are *the* Classical singer!"

KARL RÖSSEL-MAJDAN

I remember well my impression of the young Furtwängler who, with his flowing lion's mane and enormously fiery gestures, swept his orchestra before him. The different instruments sounded like a huge, ringing organism, and my father, who then sang bass under the baton of the young Master, explained to me as a boy the greatness of orchestral art: the brass instruments represent the mineral kingdom, the wood winds come from the world of plants, animals furnish the catgut strings, membranes and ivory, and above this realm of animate and inanimate nature, human voices in their four temperaments sing out as instruments. But all this is ruled by the conductor, who represents the personality of the creator in the macrocosm, in nature as a whole, or the personality of the human spirit in the microcosm, in the human way of life. A wonderful description!

Everything mundane, humanly fallible, everything private, external and temporary loses interest in face of the eternal essence of a masterpiece and its interpretation through the genius of the artist. With this awe and reverence for the mission of Art and the artist, Frau Hilde Rössel-Majdan—in those days an ingénue at the Vienna State Opera though already having sung in oratorios internationally under Karajan and others—met Wilhelm Furtwängler for the first time. On April 7–9, 1952, the Master conducted Bach's *Saint Matthew Passion* in the Vienna Konzerthaussaal. At the last moment, one of the soloists was indisposed, and Furtwängler had Frau Rössel-Majdan sing for him at the General Rehearsal. After a few measures he put down his baton, very pleased, and said, "You will sing the *Passion* in all three performances". Before the great alto aria "Erbarme dich . . ." Furtwängler said to the young singer, "Now you can sing with all your heart, *I* shall follow *you!*" She did, and felt heaven and earth as if from his inspiration; and the public followed her. After this Furtwängler engaged her often. There were many triumphs. But in her piano score even today, Furtwängler's handwriting recalls that very first day: "Many thanks for the splendid *Saint Matthew Passion.*"

The older Furtwängler had more tranquil gestures when he conducted; he no longer leapt up to the podium or shook his lion's mane, and yet from him there radiated a certain power that belongs only to the great magicians of the podium. The perspective of age, which had surmounted the mannerisms of a star, made this power seem even greater; and seeing the apostle of the spirit and of the music of the spheres, one forgot the man with his physical weaknesses.

In 1953, Furtwängler led the complete *Ring* in Rome, in concert form. One day, Frau Rössel-Majdan was concentrating on her role with the piano score, in order to overcome her deep stage-fright. "What singing does to the nerves!" she thought. "Experienced professionals like Furtwängler are so fortunate!" Suddenly he appeared before her and noticed her nervousness, though no one else had done so, and said, "Do you have such terrible stage-fright as I have? The last fifteen minutes before one goes on are the worst, but then it passes". How simple and yet how great is such an admission! Furtwängler too had a heart, not merely a pump without feeling. But in his music the artist overcame the man in him and merged with the masterpiece.

DAME MYRA HESS

WILHELM Furtwängler has left us the memory of many great performances, but I shall never forget when he conducted Beethoven's *Ninth Symphony* shortly after the war. The entire programme was devoted to this one work, and it was a true re-creation of the soul and mind of the composer. In the lives of us all, there are some unique musical experiences, and for me this was one of them; a great and inspired revelation.

STANISLAW SKROWACZEWSKI

In the years 1948 to 1950, I had some occasions to meet Wilhelm Furtwängler and to see and listen to his concerts. I consider him one of the few greatest conductors we ever had. I heard him a few times during the Lucerne Festivals with the Vienna Philharmonic, and in Paris. Every performance that I heard, though sometimes even not the best ones from the technical point of view (especially when he conducted French orchestras which could not sound as he wished), had something special which I call greatness. I stopped then caring if the orchestras played together or with the best tone, or if his tempi were quite the opposite of my own ideas as a performer—rather I had the impression of "seeing" the score alive and the composer resurrected.

Then, being obliged to spend the next six years behind the Iron Curtain during the "Cold War", I lost the opportunity to hear him. How interesting it was for me to return to his recordings after this long period! I was very glad to be able to receive the same kind of "atmosphere" from the recordings that I had experienced from hearing him conduct in person, and I think what I call "atmosphere" and "greatness" is really something for me indefinable, as everything in Art is indefinable. Furtwängler never wanted to show what he was doing with the composer's score, but even in his own freedom of interpreting, I felt him always "parallel" to the works he conducted.

GOTTFRIED VON EINEM

As a schoolboy of ten, I heard Wilhelm Furtwängler for the first time. It was at a concert of the Berlin Philharmonic Orchestra in Kiel, and the program featured Stravinsky's *Firebird Suite*—my first encounter with Stravinsky. I heard Furtwängler for the last time in a Beethoven concert during the Salzburg Festival in 1954. In the years separating these two concerts, I was privileged to hear the entire Classical and Romantic repertory, many modern works and numerous operatic performances under his direction. After the completion of my studies in 1938, I lived in Berlin until the end of the war, serving as Coach at the State Opera. In these years I was a constant visitor at Furtwängler's Berlin Philharmonic Concerts. It is no exaggeration to say that I owe him a substantial part of my musical education.

After 1947, during my activity with the Salzburg Festivals, I had the opportunity of working steadily with Furtwängler until his death. Whether it was his intervention for Hindemith under the Nazi régime, or his intervention on behalf of Karajan's engagement for the Salzburg Festivals, or for the performance of modern works in them, I always had to admire his personal courage and unusual kindness. He could recognize and respect an opposing view, and he was always ready to be convinced by valid arguments. When he persisted in his own point of view, it was always because of the facts, never personal vanity or financial advantages. On one occasion, in a difficult and crucial situation, the world-renowned conductor intervened, with the full weight of his name and influence, for me—a young and still unknown composer—against political interests, as he had done in the "Hindemith Case". I shall never forget that aid from this great man and warmhearted friend, and I shall never forget the many wonderful musical impressions I owe him.

SIGMUND SPAETH

In my opinion Wilhelm Furtwängler was one of the greatest conductors of all time. I heard him frequently as Director of our New York Philharmonic Orchestra and greatly admired his work.

In the summer of 1951, I had the pleasure of meeting Mr. Furtwängler in person, at an informal evening of music in the Archbishop's Palace at Salzburg. I found him a very modest and self-effacing man, sincerely interested in the performances of his colleagues.

The following summer I was again in Salzburg and had the privilege of hearing what to me was the finest production of Mozart's *Marriage of Figaro* in my experience. It had been prepared by Furtwängler, although he was too ill to conduct the actual performance that I attended. The cast included George London as the Count, Erich Kunz as Figaro, Elisabeth Schwarzkopf as the Countess, Irmgard Seefried as Susannah and Hilde Gueden as Cherubino. Furtwängler's death, not long after, was truly a tragedy.

SENA JURINAC

I deeply regret that I so rarely had the opportunity to sing under Wilhelm Furtwängler's baton: as Marzelline in *Fidelio* at the Theatre an der Wien, a production which was later recorded; and as the First Rhine Maiden, the Third Norn, and Gutrune in a radio performance of the complete *Ring of the Nibelungs*. These few times when I had the distinction of working with Dr. Furtwängler were a great experience for me. I am sorry that I do not have the literary gifts to express in the right words the deep impression he made on me, yet, rare as they were, I shall always remember our meetings with deepest gratitude.

GINA BACHAUER

I never had the privilege of playing under Wilhelm Furtwängler, but I heard him conduct many performances in London, Paris, and other cities. It was always a wonderful experience to hear him because, whether one agreed with his interpretation or not, his musicianship and intense personality, together with his sincerity towards the music, commanded great respect.

I well remember being present at the H. M.V. recording studios in London some years ago when Yehudi Menuhin was recording the Bartók *Violin Concerto* with Furtwängler: I was full of admiration for the infinite amount of trouble Furtwängler took in adjusting even the smallest details of balance and musical phrasing. The world has undoubtedly been enriched by his devoted contribution to music.

COLIN DAVIS

I hate to admit it, but I never saw Furtwängler in action, and only know his gramophone records. I find his disturbance of momentum in the Classical works unconvincing: one can see what he is trying to do, but that he ever thought this was the way to do it, seems incomprehensible. Yet from the evidence of his recordings, when on his best form, he was the greatest conductor of his generation—I suppose this means that he conducted works the way I like them to go!

MANOUG PARIKIAN

Concertmaster, Philharmonia Orchestra of London, 1949–1957

My impressions of Wilhelm Furtwängler must necessarily be confined to the last four years of his life. His first concert with the Philharmonia was in May 1950, and his last (and perhaps most memorable) concert in 1954. This was the Beethoven *Choral Symphony*, which we played twice at that year's Festival in Lucerne. I think he must have been particularly happy with these performances, because I remember how warmly he shook my hand in the Artists' Room afterwards, thus to express his gratitude to the members of the Philharmonia Orchestra. In my opinion these two performances and the complete recording of *Tristan and Isolde* were the highlights of his appearances with us. The *Tristan* recording in particular has left a lasting impression on me, in spite of the fact that I do not normally enjoy Wagner's operas. For this reason I was not very enthusiastic about the prospect of recording *Tristan*, which took three weeks. But when I look back on eight years' association with the Philharmonia, most of it spent in the recording studio, I remember those three weeks as some of the most enjoyable of all. Furtwängler was absolute master in the studio from beginning till the end, and his singleness of purpose was remarkable. I particularly remember the way he took advantage of the then new process of tape-recording, by playing whole stretches of the opera without stopping to correct minor mistakes. He was impatient with anybody who interfered with the continuity of his thoughts and of the performance. He did actually once walk out of the studio in a rage. There was still half an hour of the session to go, but he did not return that day.

I find it difficult to remember details about his conducting or his personality; perhaps in saying this I have unwittingly summed up the essence of his artistry. One had to consider the performance as a whole, rather than details of phrasing or accentuation, to do justice to his interpretations.

From my position as leader of the Orchestra I sometimes felt unduly worried about details which he did not seem to notice. I do not think this mattered very much, even though it made one's job a little more difficult. However, I entirely disagree with those who maintain that his beat was uncertain and unclear. I know more than one story about this aspect of Furtwängler's conducting technique ("Start playing when his stick reaches the third button of his waistcoat" etc. etc.). But I always found his beat firm and eloquent. On one occasion he sensed that the strings would have liked a firmer up-beat. He stopped and explained, rather impatiently, that he could, if he wanted, give a perfectly clear beat—and showed it to us. But, he said, "That is not the effect I want". Another important point: even when you let your attention wander away from his beat for a moment you always returned to it and found it where you expected it to be, in a given bar or phrase. This was true, in spite of the fact that he treated each phrase with considerable rhythmic license. Even his changes of tempo had a certain logical and very musical shape and continuity, and he always allowed the music to breathe, to live and to sing. That was, perhaps, only one of his qualities. But it was a significant one, which placed him above most conductors of his day.

BLANCHE THEBOM

My one experience with Maestro Furtwängler was in London at the time of the recording of the complete *Tristan* with Kirsten Flagstad. Although I had by that time sung the role of Brangaene many, many times, I found myself continually surprised and delighted with what seemed almost a new score to me.

Furtwängler had the assurance and the courage to take slower tempi than I had ever previously heard. I shall never forget the measures in the first act during which Brangaene approaches Tristan for the first time with her message from Isolde. In the hurried and nervous renditions with which I was familiar this passage had always seemed to me to be a martial air—but it suddenly emerged as I am now convinced Wagner meant it, as the welling surge and drop of the ship over and into the troughs of the waves.

I regret that I had only one opportunity to work with Furtwängler, but am grateful to a kind fate which made this memorable experience possible.

GYORGY SANDOR

I shall be more than happy to add a word to the many said in praise and recognition of this musical giant, whose powerful and original interpretations have inspired so many of us. It is interesting that this invitation reached me in Vienna, where I happened to attend one of Furtwängler's last concerts, a memorable performance of the Bach *Saint Matthew Passion*, shortly before he passed away. His health was failing already, but this certainly did not impair the intensity of his creative genius. I am using the word "creative" on purpose, since he seemed to be able to bring to life more of the essence of Music than any other conductor I have known. This was my impression when I heard him on another most memorable occasion too, at the first concert he conducted in London after World War II, with the Berlin Philharmonic under his baton. The men did not wear formal attire, since they did not own any in those days, but there was a Brahms *Fourth Symphony* to remember always, and a Beethoven *Fourth Piano Concerto*, where Dame Myra Hess and Furtwängler were worthy companions of Beethoven. There were fourteen thousand people at Empress Hall to cheer them.

LUDWIG SUTHAUS

Dᴜʀɪɴɢ our years of music-making together, I was very close to Dr. Furtwängler. Wherever it was—Rome, London, Berlin— I was always the tenor he expected. He was the last great Romantic among conductors, and until now he has found no true successor. His tempi were broad, and he knew how to convey them as no one else could. He made the greatest demands on his singers, yet when one understood him, everything was easy.

I shall never forget the recording sessions for *Tristan* in London: eighteen days, six hours of recording a day. Furtwängler dreamed of making a recording which would give the listener the impression of a performance in the opera house, and so we singers had to sing out over the large Wagner orchestra exactly as in a live performance. Long sections were repeated as many as six times. It was the same in the recording sessions for *Walküre* in October 1954, the last time I was privileged to work with him. How fatherly his advice, not to drive too fast in my auto, for he still had so many things he wished to do with me. But it was his auto that drove the faster. His death drove a breach in the ranks of the Great which has not yet been closed.

ENRICO MAINARDI

I met Furtwängler in Berlin, in 1925. These were the years when that city was still the musical center of Europe. The concerts conducted by Furtwängler were the most important and most moving events of the season. Unforgettable were the performances of the Berlin Philharmonic Orchestra, of great soloists under the guidance of the ingenious conductor; a public cultivated and passionate for music, especially the one at the General Rehearsal on Sunday mornings, crowded the glorious old *Philharmonie* to listen with devotion and boundless enthusiasm.

I first had the opportunity to play under Furtwängler in 1933, during the celebration of the Brahms Centenary, when I performed the *Double Concerto* with Georg Kulenkampff in Berlin and Hamburg. Later he invited me to play the Schumann *Concerto* with him in Berlin; how fervently he supported and inspired his soloist! On other occasions I was fortunate to play under him at La Scala, Turin, the Lucerne and Edinburgh Festivals, and I remember all these concerts with gratitude.

As I write these brief notes, so many moments lived beside this musician and artist come back to my mind, this noble figure before me, with his profound, blue, dreaming eyes. . . . Conversation with him was always stimulating and fruitful, free from any pose or affectation, whatever the subject; his vast culture and rare, acute sensitivity enabled him to speak interestingly on any subject in a very personal way. In spite of some outward appearances which could be misunderstood by a superficial observer, the modesty of this artist was sincere: he was certainly aware of his own value, yet conscious of the duty and the privilege which Destiny had given him—to give the greatest and most genuine interpretations of German music, to transmit its noble message, to revive it for the people who felt the need for it and looked for consolation in the realm of sound. And yet what a tormented life his was! Perhaps a torment harsher than the one we all must accept, because of the inexorable aggravation of deafness in the last years of his life.

Among my memories illuminating the character of Furtwängler, I wish to mention in particular a moving episode that took place a few years after World War II. After a long pause in his activity as conductor—a forced and absurd pause which had exasperated and gravely troubled him—I arranged that the Santa Cecilia Academy in Rome invite him to conduct. The Academy was honored in inviting him before any other musical society, to give two concerts, which the Roman public heard with indescribable rapture. I was very close to him in those days, and I attended all his rehearsals. At the first one, as he excitedly and impatiently prepared to mount the podium of the Theatro Adriano where the Orchestra was anxiously awaiting him, he hesitated for a moment and asked me, "Shall I still know how to conduct?" No less excited than he, I gave him an affectionate push that started him toward his position before the Orchestra, welcomed by warm applause. And then the rehearsal began: the Brahms *First Symphony*. After fifteen minutes, the Roman Orchestra of Santa Cecilia, almost hypnotized by Furtwängler's magic baton, sounded like his own Berlin Philharmonic. During these minutes he had not said one word: such was the communicative and artistic power of this musician! One of his secrets, or rather peculiarities, was to speak very little or not at all during rehearsals. He assured me that when something did not quite satisfy him, first of all he looked for the error within himself and in his gesture: once he had corrected himself, in most cases the orchestra yielded what he wished, what no word could have obtained.

It was the power of persuasion, the expression of his gestures, and the instinct for purity and truth that moulded his wishes and obliged every member of the orchestra to follow him in order to fulfill them. The gestures which caused so many discussions, even occasional ironic remarks, which no one could ever define, much less imitate, were able to draw incomparable results out of the orchestra. If his technique of conducting was individual and very personal, what distinguished Furtwängler from all others was his search for the secret of a composition, its spiritual basis, its imponderable meaning, and his communication of these to the listener, however ill-prepared. By discovering the *inneren Plan*, as he used to say, by obtaining balance and harmony between form and content—this is the way Furtwängler sought and found fidelity to the spirit of the works, in themselves, rather than in the superficial observance of the conventional indications of the text: for these are not always sufficient to reveal the most profound, transcendent intentions of the composer, due to the natural and intrinsic limitations of a word or sign in the magical world of music.

The tempo, the long, breathing phrases, the intimate passion, the Leonardian "precise weight" of his performances placed in bright and clear light the hidden meaning, the substance, the expression of all the works he interpreted—not only German works: his *Otello* was a revelation!—and often made the listener feel that Furtwängler's way of conducting them was the only true and valid one. The fact that he was himself a composer undoubtedly aided his successful penetration into the psychic and formal problems of the music he interpreted. For him, as for all great artists, technical perfection was a means and not an end;

he avoided excessively prepared performances, maintaining that one should reserve a margin for improvisation, for intuition, for the charm of the moment, a margin for ecstasy and creative imagination.

There is still another Roman episode I wish to relate. We had not seen each other for a long time; since I was staying in Rome for a few days while he was conducting there, I took the opportunity to be with him several times. During one of our talks he expressed himself more bitterly than usual, about the world situation in general and his own in particular; he was very disturbed and depressed by a feeling of loneliness and isolation. He felt himself, he said sadly, increasingly uprooted, offended by the style and *mores* in our world of artists, and by the way of life in recent times. I tried to calm him, to persuade him that in spite of discouraging appearances, there was still a great deal of good worth saving in this confused world of ours; and I made him recall how a large public in every musical center welcomed him with recognition, unusual warmth, and exceptional admiration.

"Yes, it is true", he replied, "but an artist needs something else. The public today applauds everything and everybody, often without making any distinction, and perhaps it applauds me for precisely the wrong reasons". Shortly thereafter he confessed to me in all seriousness, "My dear, if I had known thirty years ago what I know now, I should *really* have become a great conductor". "A pity", I said with equal seriousness, "a real pity, Herr Doktor! We have, alas, missed forever a really great conductor. Patience!". This made him laugh heartily.

We left then, and I accompanied him, since he had to present himself at the Vatican to be received by Pope Pius XII. For an hour we walked through the sunny streets and byways of Rome. Along the whole route he directed an invisible orchestra, trying to explain how the attack of the Beethoven *Fifth Symphony* had always preoccupied him; he had conducted it marvelously just the day before at the Theatro dell'Argentina. He explained that no matter how many ways there were of conducting the beginning, in reality there was only one valid way which fulfilled its drama and expressive power, and added his reasons for this conviction. Those who listened to the way Furtwängler began this symphony can realize what he meant by his emphatic statement.

Around us amazed but respectful pedestrians looked at this unusual figure who walked along singing and making gestures, and they intuitively guessed that he was a fanatic musician. A few, recognizing him, smiled kindly, as if to an old friend. The only one who did not notice anything, of course, was Furtwängler himself, whom I left at the end of this musical walk before the solemn entrance of the Vatican.

Other characteristic traits of his honesty and candor were the total lack of exhibitionism, the great simplicity of his ways, and his indifference to material things—sometimes necessary even for a great artist.

Dramatically, painfully, his death has left in all of us a void that cannot be refilled.

Aware that he was dying, until the last moment he tried to console his adored wife Elisabeth, assuring her that he was serene and awaited death as a liberation.

My good friend Wilhelm, I believe that Divine Providence, in spite of all, was kind, and wished to spare you even greater bitterness and disillusion in a world which had become so different from the one we dreamed of and loved all our lives as artists.

I shall close now, recalling the last concert he conducted at the Lucerne Festival a few months before his death. On the program was the Bruckner *Seventh Symphony*—purified, heavenly, transfigured! *As if he knew* that this would be his last performance of that work.

We, your friends, shall never forget the musical miracle, the consuming drama of that farewell between a great composer and his interpreter, a farewell to earthly life with its vibrant message of deep and luminous humanity!

IGOR MARKEVITCH

CIRCUMSTANCES brought me to be the first to conduct the Berlin Philharmonic Orchestra after Furtwängler's death. A few days before, I had met some of these musicians at the funeral of that remarkable man. We had thus been able to talk about him, and I gathered the feeling of what his death had meant to them. They were like a family which had lost its father. The musicians talked of him with a tender affection and a gratefulness one rarely meets. They often told me that when they worked with him, he managed to make them feel above themselves. Furtwängler knew, with a magnificent simplicity, how to make people understand the deeper meanings of things.

His greatest gift was to create an atmosphere in which he communicated a love of music and the respect he had for the thought of the masters. One also felt this when one talked to him, and his conversation was always enriching. Furtwängler put you in contact with a great tradition which he managed to keep alive. I was particularly struck by this one day when he analyzed with me the meaning of Haydn's work. He understood its importance with a refinement and a culture which brought out in him the mark of a deep European civilization. That is how I remember him: a wonderfully civilized man, a man one loved for being a mixture of greatness and true modesty.

YEHUDI MENUHIN

Address opening the "Furtwängler Festival" on WBAI-FM, New York,
January 25, 1960

I welcome this opportunity of associating myself with Furtwängler in this great city of New York, where I had hoped some
years ago to be with him on the stage of Carnegie Hall. It is sad
that he died just a few months too soon to realize his and my
ambition of bringing together the musical public of New York
with the great music that he could conduct so remarkably. It is
perhaps characteristic of human destiny that the timing of those
things we most desire eludes us. The moments that we hope for
come just a little bit too late, when those who are most concerned
can no longer enjoy them. But that is an essential part of continuity, for if everything happened at the right time, there would
be no time at all. In other words, things would end when they
were meant to continue. Now Furtwängler is still with us, thanks
to the miracle of recordings. He did live long enough to bequeath
us his interpretations on tape. What we are about to play is not
recorded on the very latest stereo tape, but during the last years
of his life recording had already reached a very, very high degree
of excellence. There are plenty of higher frequencies and lower
frequencies, but to my mind these refinements of reproduction
are not the very essence and core of music. They help, they give
the illusion, they are a "more perfect mirror", if you wish, but
still the real part of music remains the interpretation, the conception, the way it is put over, and the communication which it
effects with the listener. That is achieved in these recordings, I
feel, in a way which can hardly be improved upon by any device
of the recording technique.

I should like to say a few words about Furtwängler's own attitude to music. Once, in Lucerne, he compared the sequence, the continuity of a work with the flow of a river as the same water went through a changing countryside, changed its path, its tempo, sometimes roaring through a narrow gulch and sometimes widening out to a flat, quiet, stately pace—thus thinking of it always as something which lived, and of which the essential momentum had to be carried on, which could not be arbitrarily changed, interrupted, halted, "pushed around"; and this same attitude of respecting the living work of music—for music is essentially something which happens in time, as the growth of an animal or a tree—this respect for the living continuity of a piece of music was very deep in Furtwängler and showed itself in the very way he conducted. There was nothing arbitrary about his conducting: in fact, he resisted the desire to dot the i's and cross the t's, and he did not want to impose too stern or too rigid a frame upon his musicians. He preferred to start the piece and let something happen. You were always sure with a Furtwängler interpretation that the magic, if there was any magic to come, would not be barred from the performance, that that intangible inspiration would not meet with a frozen, locked gate such as too often happens with interpretations that are completely and coldly conceived mechanically. Whenever he began conducting, he was in another dimension, in fact he really lived for the most part in that "dream world of music" and reluctantly was dragged out of it whenever things of the ordinary life, the routine, and whatever it may have been, forced themselves upon his attention. He was in fact a different man when he had to deal with the minor irritations of life from when he was in front of an orchestra.

I was interested to read the other day that Bernard Berenson, whom I had the great privilege of knowing quite well, once wrote an article about the degree to which a particular style of art is dependent upon the impediments of an artist. There is no doubt that it is the very obstacles and the very difficulties we have to overcome which form to a large degree our style, and in Furtwängler whatever it was that prevented him from being the kind of conductor that, let us say, Fritz Reiner is—a very great conductor, a very effective one—those were the very qualities which evolved a different order of things, a kind of approach which had its own value, its own justification. When you have one hundred people playing for you—good musicians—you are not conducting one person, you are conducting the sum total of many different approaches to music. Something happens that makes the total reaction of an intelligent body of musicians more valid and more right than that of any single one of them. Especially is this true when the work is a Classical work in which they are deeply steeped, of which they know the tradition very well. I have always found that a whole orchestra is never wrong. It is a remarkable phenomenon that this body of musicians, once they have grown together and established their *rapport*, can be trusted to continue playing in a certain style and in a certain way, to breathe at the right points, to follow the curve of a phrase in the right way; and the importance of the conductor is to guide them as a very wonderful rider might guide a horse, which is an intelligent being. It is an entirely different matter from driving a car, which is not an intelligent being. Most of the current approach, shall we say, "the contemporary approach", has been the attitude that one takes to a motor car: one wants the most perfect instrument that will have immediate response, that will have the quickest getaway, that will stop within inches, and so on. This is the kind of orchestra that many conductors have produced; but I feel there is another dimension, that conducting an orchestra, as I have seen Furtwängler do, is more like riding an intelligent horse, which already knows a great deal and needs only an understanding with the rider, a real friendship which may have grown up over many years so that each trusts the other. This is much more like the way Furtwängler conducted and more like his attitude than that of many of the conductors I know. This was the inspiration he gave his musicians and his soloists.

I have had to say all this, whereas if we had played in Carnegie Hall a few years ago it would have been quite unnecessary. I should merely have played with him, and the audience would have understood all this quite instinctively and without the need of any words. Let us hope that even this intangible medium which comes over the waves of the air from this radio station will nonetheless convey something of that magic through his recordings. I am happy to have had this moment to speak about Furtwängler in New York City.

v

MICHAEL MARCUS

Furtwängler on Record

I MUST confess that when I agreed to undertake a discography for this memorial volume I thought that the task was fairly straight-forward. However, the past year has seen the release of more Furtwängler recordings than ever before, perhaps a greater quantity than at any period during his life, and it seems that future releases are still likely for some time to come. I realize that the following guide is not quite complete, but I hope there will be the opportunity to revise it and bring it up to date in the light of forthcoming releases. I have tried at various points to give some indication of what should be issued in the future, drawing upon the list of Furtwängler's Berlin concerts published by F. A. Brockhaus, Wiesbaden, in 1958, under the title *Wilhelm Furtwängler. Die Programme der Konzerte mit dem Berliner Philharmonischen Orchester 1922–1954.* Many wartime concerts have been preserved on wire recordings, and those from postwar years exist on tape in the various Berlin radio stations.

Unfortunately there are many gaps in the recorded legacy of Furtwängler. Tapes of his Beethoven *Second* and *Eighth Symphonies*, the Bruckner *Fourth* and *Fifth* from his concerts, and those from his Salzburg performances of *Die Zauberflöte, Don Giovanni, Otello* and other operas should be made available on records. The opportunities are endless.

My thanks are due to Electrical and Musical Industries Limited and the Deutsche Grammophon Gesellschaft for supplying me with re-cordings which I would otherwise not have heard. For the most part, I have noted only English, German and American pressings.

BACH: *Brandenburg Concerto No. 3 in G.* Berlin Philharmonic Orchestra. Polydor 95417–8, reissued DGG EPL 30539 (45 rpm).

I tend to be a purist where the *Third Brandenburg* is concerned. I like to hear an interpolated middle movement to fill out two linking chords, and I prefer the texture provided by the nine solo strings specified by Bach. Furtwängler uses a full body of strings and no continuo, and adopts tempi which might fairly be described as stately. Despite the size of the forces involved and the age of the recording, he achieves a surprising degree of clarity, and his rhythmic control is always vital and alive. However, I cannot say that I care for the results, and I cannot help wondering whether Furtwängler would ever have modified his approach, following modern scholarship, because his feeling for the music itself is undoubtedly sympathetic. The transfer has been well managed, though the second side has a higher degree of surface hiss than the first.

BACH: *Suite No. 3 in D.* Berlin Philharmonic Orchestra. DGG 18856; also in KL 27–31. *Air in G* only. Berlin Philharmonic Orchestra. Polydor 66926 or 66935, reissued DGG EPL 30164 (45 rpm).

The complete *Suite* dates from a concert in October 1948, and it is a pity that the recording is not more satisfactory. Like the Mozart 39 with which it is coupled on the LP, the sound is boomy and bass heavy, and the detail does not emerge with the clarity one would like. The *Overture* is where the performance suffers most from the tonal deficiencies, but subsequently the dance movements come over quite well, with Furtwängler's lightness of touch well in evidence. If the Bach style is not as delicate as seems to be the fashion today, Furtwängler's good-humoured, indeed at times rumbustious, approach would probably have earned the approval of the Cantor himself. There is much to enjoy here, and those acquiring the album will discover the delights of the performance in due course. The early account of the *Air* was originally the fill-up to the *Midsummer Night's Dream Overture*, but has been coupled with the *Rosamunde G major Ballet Music* for its reissue on EP. It is useful to have this for the sake of completeness, but otherwise its interest is largely historical. A Berlin performance of the *Second Suite* from February 1953 might well be worth issuing, particularly as Aurèle Nicolet was the flautist.

BARTÓK: *Violin Concerto No. 2 (1938)*. Yehudi Menuhin, soloist. Philharmonia Orchestra. HMV ALP 1121; Electrola E 90070.

"Because I feel it that way", Furtwängler is reputed to have replied to an enquiry from Bartók as to why he played a particular passage the way he did. Whether or not Furtwängler conducted the *Violin Concerto* because he felt it that way I cannot say, but this middle one of Menuhin's three recordings of the *Concerto* eloquently demonstrates that Furtwängler's renown as a conductor of contemporary scores was thoroughly deserved. His organizational skills in manipulating the material is reflected in the shapely way the outer movements hang together. Furtwängler's attention to concerto form is as strict here as in any Classical concerto and if the music sounds possibly less rhapsodic than usual, it gains in strength and dignity. Furtwängler's command of the rhythms is as crisp and lively as that of any compatriot of the composer, as the account of the Finale readily shows. Menuhin, of course, was usually found at his most inspired when playing with Furtwängler, and this recording is no exception. A Berlin tape of the *Concerto for Orchestra* exists, but I have not heard it. Made in October 1950, it would be a valuable document.

BEETHOVEN: *Coriolan Overture*. Vienna Philharmonic Orchestra. HMV DB 6625 (del.).

As far as I can trace, this performance seems never to have been transferred to LP, or even EP, anywhere at all. There may be some reason for this, but I cannot imagine why it should have been thus neglected, unless the master has been broken or there is some similar technical reason. The performance is good, broad and powerful, with the tragic atmosphere of the piece always brooding over the whole design. The recording is marred by excessive artificial echo, and there is consequently some blurring of the wood-wind detail, but the effect of the performance is still impressive. This is the only Furtwängler *Coriolan* we are likely to have; the Berlin concerts do not show anything from which a tape could have been made, but perhaps there is something elsewhere.

BEETHOVEN: *Fidelio*. Martha Mödl (Leonore), Wolfgang Windgassen (Florestan), Otto Edelmann (Don Pizarro), Sena Jurinac (Marzelline), Gottlob Frick (Rocco), Alfred Poell (Don Fernando). Vienna Philharmonic Orchestra and Chorus of the Vienna State Opera. HMV ALP 1130–2; Electrola E 90071–3.

We are told that this album was recorded immediately after the last of a special series of *Fidelio* performances which took place in Vienna in the late Autumn of 1953. I understand that some sessions, if not all, did actually take place during the same night, and tiredness took its inevitable toll of the singers. Indeed, this is not entirely the recording of *Fidelio* we had every right to expect from Furtwängler. However, despite the fact that the singers are not always up to their parts and the lack of spoken dialogue, there are moments of insight in the handling of the orchestra which make this set indispensable. The whiplash of the strings in Pizzaro's entrance aria, the sinister atmosphere evoked in the dungeon scene, and the heaven-storming grandeur of the Finale are but some instances of the profound understanding of Beethoven displayed here. Surprisingly, however, Furtwängler is less moving in the Prisoners' Chorus than one would expect, and certainly this episode does not match the sublime account he gave of it in Salzburg in 1950. For that matter, the *Leonore No. 3* given here is but a pale shadow of the 1950 performance I heard, which kept the audience cheering for twenty minutes. Nevertheless, it is useful to have this overture reasonably well preserved. The recording is good, and the lack of stereo none too distressing. A generous disc of highlights is available on Electrola E 80038 for those who may wish to investigate the performance.

BEETHOVEN: *Grosse Fugue in B flat, Op. 133. Egmont Overture. Leonore Overture No. 2, Op. 72a.* Berlin Philharmonic Orchestra. DGG LPM 18859.

I am not at all certain that playing the *Grosse Fugue* with a full body of strings enhances the stature of the piece, since the effort that four players have to put into the music becomes dissipated when spread over orchestral forces. The guiding influence of Furtwängler certainly helps to bring out the force of Beethoven's inspiration, and he also reveals far greater variety of colour and texture than is possible with a string quartet. But even he cannot prevent there being some loss of tension and cumulative dramatic force in the central section where in the string quartet version the very impulse of the players and their sense of struggle carries the music forward. The massed Berlin strings play wonderfully well, with every inflection in place, but there is a slight touch of academicism about the result. Nevertheless, this is interesting for the evidence it offers that Furtwängler was completely attuned to Beethoven's thought no matter what sphere the composer was working in. The versions of *Egmont* and *Leonore No. 2* are the same as those filling out the DGG recordings of the *Fifth* and *Fourth Symphonies,* so that the acquisition of this record will result in some duplication; but the *Grosse Fugue* is well worth having. The recording is rich.

BEETHOVEN: *Leonore Overture No. 2*. Berlin Philharmonic Orchestra. HMV ALP 1324 (del.); Electrola E 70421. DGG LPM 18742.

The HMV and DGG performances of *No. 2* are not the same, while the *No. 3* comes from the complete *Fidelio* recording. The DGG version fills out a recording of the *Fourth Symphony* and has a rather constricted sound, but the stature of the reading shines through. The HMV one is a marvel, for the interpretation translates the work into a masterpiece in its own right, an achievement which can be fully appreciated on the Electrola 10-inch disc where it is sensibly coupled with *No. 3*. As I mentioned, this account of the latter does not quite attain the blazing fervour of Furtwängler's performance in Salzburg in 1950, but it has much to commend, and it helps to fill out our view of Furtwängler as a Beethoven interpreter. Both recordings are good, that of the HMV *No. 2* in particular is one of the best Furtwängler ever received.

BEETHOVEN: *Piano Concerto No. 5 in E flat, Op. 73, "Emperor"*. Edwin Fischer, soloist. Philharmonia Orchestra. HMV ALP 1051; Electrola E 90048; also in EBE 600000 1–6 (Electronic Stereo).

"Magisterial" is the word that immediately springs to mind when listening to this performance. Fischer and Furtwängler were like-minded musicians, and together they bring to the *Emperor Concerto* an immense stride, power and dignity. Furtwängler's launching of the opening tutti is of unparalleled magnificence, his shaping of the slow movement unmatched in its eloquence, and the rhythmic spring of the Finale superbly exhilarating. Fischer's phrasing is dovetailed with the accompaniment in an expressive manner, and even though his technique is tested beyond its limits in one or two places, these minor blemishes do not affect the impact of this stupendous performance. The recording, particularly on recent HMV pressings, still sounds clear and full-bodied, but I find the Electronic Stereo effort dull and lacking in presence.

BEETHOVEN: *Symphony No. 1 in C, Op. 21*. Vienna Philharmonic Orchestra. HMV ALP 1324 (del.); Electrola E 60657.

This was the last work to be conducted by Furtwängler in the series of Berlin Philharmonic concerts which began in 1922. The programme of September 19 and 20, 1954, consisted of only two works, the conductor's *Second Symphony* and Beethoven's *First*. Although the public performance might well be included in any future memorial editions, it is not really necessary, for this recording is excellent. In his reading Furtwängler perfectly relates style and content, on the one hand taking into full account the work's Mozartian influences and, on the other, looking ahead to the greater things to come. The bounds of the music are never burst, and the moods and emotions always remain within the framework set by Beethoven. The Finale receives a performance at least as spirited as those of other conductors more renowned for dynamism than Furtwängler was, and the whole moulding of the work betokens the master hand. The playing is first-class and the recording admirable.

BEETHOVEN: *Symphony No. 3 in E flat, Op. 55, "Eroica"*. Vienna Philharmonic Orchestra. HMV DB 6741–7 (del.). Vienna Philharmonic Orchestra. HMV ALP 1060; Electrola E 90050; also in EBE 600000 1–6 (Electronic Stereo). Vienna Philharmonic Orchestra. Urania URLP 7095 (del.).

The HMV LP will have to serve as the standard Furtwängler recording of the *Eroica*. Good as it is, and it is very fine, I have heard better from him in the concert hall and on broadcasts, particularly one from Paris when on a tour with the Berlin Philharmonic. Some idea of the sheer excitement that Furtwängler could evoke from the score comes through the murky sound of the Urania disc. The origins of this performance are not very clear; it could have been a pirated tape, and Furtwängler did succeed in having it suppressed by the courts, but it has a lift and impact that capture something of the white heat of a live Furtwängler performance. The sound on the HMV LP is excellent, especially in the latest pressings, and is quite superior to the Electronic Stereo disc. The performance is a great one. Here Furtwängler shows incomparably how to extract the utmost meaning from any phrase while never losing sight of the over-all design. The lead into the coda of the first movement is a masterpiece of sustained and controlled tension, and in the coda itself the giant stride of the composer's imagination is unforgettably unleashed. The Finale, too, is welded together with supreme force and vigour, and the Vienna Philharmonic horns are superb. The earlier HMV recording was perhaps more thoughtful, but there was no denying a certain lack of power, and the effect is inevitably a little pallid by the side of the later one. A Berlin *Eroica* led by Furtwängler in December 1952 exists on tape, and could supplement this.

BEETHOVEN: *Symphony No. 4 in B flat, Op. 60*. Vienna Philharmonic Orchestra. HMV DB 21099–103. Vienna Philharmonic Orchestra. HMV ALP 1059 (del.); Electrola E 90049. Berlin Philharmonic Orchestra. DGG LPM 18817; DGG LPM 18742.

As with the *Eroica*, the HMV 78s and the LP are not the same performance. The DGG is taken from a concert in Berlin. I have the feeling that Furtwängler was capable of a finer Beethoven *Fourth* than he put on record. Admittedly the eloquence of the slow movement remains unequalled, particularly in the HMV LP version, but I find the Scherzo distinctly lacking in brio on each occasion, and the allegro of the first movement is not guided with absolute certainty towards its final goal. I cannot understand why he omits the repeat in this movement. This is, of course, judging the performances by the highest Furtwängler standards, and from anyone else we would hail any of these performances as marvels of eloquent expressiveness. The gulf that separates even not quite the greatest of Furtwängler from his rivals is shown when one compares, say, the DGG performance with Jochum's, an interpretation on very much the same lines as Furtwängler's, but without the inner meaning in every phrase which makes one attend to Furtwängler even when disagreeing with him. The HMV LP is the best-recorded version, but it is not without some echo and a slight unsteadiness in fortissimo passages. Nevertheless it is an important contribution to the Furtwängler Beethoven canon.

BEETHOVEN: *Symphony No. 5 in C minor, Op. 67.* Berlin Philharmonic Orchestra. HMV DB 3328–32. Vienna Philharmonic Orchestra. HMV ALP 1195; Electrola E 90088; also in EBE 600000 1–6 (Electronic Stereo). Berlin Philharmonic Orchestra. DGG LPM 18724.

Since the late thirties the HMV Berlin set has reigned as the classic version of the *C minor Symphony* on record. It was Furtwängler's first HMV recording, and he brought to the music the full impact of his inspiration at its peak. The outer movements are strong and firm, full of a transcendent nobility and fervour which have irresistible sweep. The middle movements are shaped with an appreciation of the underlying Romantic content, and the effect is enhanced by the eloquent playing of the Berlin Philharmonic. This performance will soon be reissued in the Great Recordings of the Century Series, an accolade it richly deserves. The fervour of this approach is carried to even greater lengths in the DGG performance, taken from his first postwar concert in Berlin. The stride and stature of the reading are undeniable, but perhaps a little repose here and there would have helped the over-all impression even more. There is still another recording of the *Fifth* by Furtwängler and his Berlin musicians, made in 1927. It is understood to be his very first recording and is of interest for that reason, as well as for the tempi chosen by the conductor as a younger man.

I like the Vienna performance very much. It has been criticized for its slow pacing, yet there is no lack of tension, and Furtwängler's judgment of weight and climax is as certain as ever. The main feeling here is of majesty and dignity, which are by no means inappropriate to the symphony. The music is always moving forward, and there is none of the laboured, halting progress that disfigures the equally slow or slower Kleiber performance. It is the best-recorded version of Furtwängler's *Fifth*, and the smooth, weighty sound aptly matches the performance. All the available editions are well worth careful study to see how Furtwängler's approach to Beethoven developed.

BEETHOVEN: *Symphony No. 6 in F, Op. 68, "Pastoral"*. Vienna Philharmonic Orchestra. HMV ALP 1041; Electrola E 90040.

Many have objected to the slow tempo for the first movement in this performance, yet surely if you are out taking a stroll through the countryside you are not galloping madly along but are taking in the sights and pleasures of the scene. Within this context, Furtwängler's speed is eminently satisfactory, for the phrasing of the main subject is shapely and graceful, and the pulse, as always, fluent and firm. No one can surpass Furtwängler in bringing out the melodic beauty that lies hidden in the lower strings in the slow movement, and certainly the Peasants go about their lawful occasions with considerably more spirit than on another recording by a celebrated German conductor that has been much admired. Furtwängler realizes that the Storm is simply a stylized storm and not meant as an accurate portrayal of the power of Nature, and he brings an appropriate feeling of benediction to the Thanksgiving. The Vienna Philharmonic rarely played better for him, and the recording reproduces the performance with a wonderfully rich sonority. Whether a tape of the Berlin performance of May 1954 would produce a superior performance is problematic. I should doubt it.

BEETHOVEN: *Symphony No. 7 in A, Op. 92.* Vienna Philharmonic Orchestra. HMV DB 21106–10; Electrola E 90016.

This is not quite the finest statement of the *Seventh* by Furtwängler that I have heard; at least one Salzburg and one Festival Hall performance were superior. It is nevertheless a transcendent reading. This is particularly true of the Allegretto, where Furtwängler searches out the inner meaning of the music in a manner unequalled on disc. The sheer poignancy of the phrasing of the second subject is moving in its direct intensity, and the orchestra responds to Furtwängler's inspiration with playing of surpassing beauty. A hearing of the outer movements should be enough to convince the doubters that the theory that Furtwängler was addicted to slow tempi, especially in Beethoven, is a slander. The rhythm of the first movement's allegro is controlled with a force and vigour that bring out the forward impulse of the music irresistibly, while the Dionysiac fury of the Finale is overwhelming. In the two live performances I mentioned Furtwängler kept an even stricter control on the basic tempo; here the final pages do tend towards the hectic, but the result is so exciting that it is a fault easily overlooked. The recording in the Electrola transfer is a little raucous in climaxes, but the tone is generally solid and there is much detail. It is surprising that the recording has never been made available on LP in England.

BEETHOVEN: *Symphony No. 9 in D Minor, Op. 125, "Choral"*. Elisabeth Schwarzkopf, Elisabeth Höngen, Hans Hopf, Otto Edelmann, soloists. Bayreuth Festival Chorus and Orchestra (1951). HMV ALP 1286–7; Electrola E 90015–6; Angel GRB 4003.

It is a tragedy that this is the only recording of the *Choral* by Furtwängler we have. Even though the performance is fine enough to enable one to appreciate Furtwängler's grasp of the music, the technically flawed playing is not altogether worthy of his memory. If he had been working with an orchestra more accustomed to his methods, the results would undoubtedly have been even more sublime than they, in fact, are; but the Bayreuth Orchestra does perform valiantly. Tapes exist of the 1950 and 1951 Berlin performances, but the reading that we really want on record is the stupendous Lucerne performance of 1954, when the orchestra was the Philharmonia. I understand that Swiss Musicians' Union rules may prevent this ever seeing the light of day, but it would be wonderful to have it.

In the present recording, from the brooding opening of the first movement, through the massive stride of the Scherzo and the wonderfully sustained cantabile of the slow movement, to the final outburst of jubilation, Furtwängler holds us enthralled. No other recorded performance of the slow movement quite matches this one, and Furtwängler's penetration of the music's innermost secrets is likely to remain unparalleled. In the Finale the soloists and chorus give him fervent support. Even Hans Hopf, not normally the most appealing of tenors, sings out with ringing confidence. In that this performance marked the opening of Bayreuth after the war, it is already a historical document; in that it is the only Furtwängler *Choral* we have, it is also a musical one.

BEETHOVEN: *Violin Concerto*. Yehudi Menuhin, soloist. Lucerne Festival Orchestra. HMV DB 6574–9 (del.). Yehudi Menuhin, soloist. Philharmonia Orchestra. HMV ALP 1100; Electrola E 90065; also in EBE 600000 1–6 (Electronic Stereo). Wolfgang Schneiderhan, soloist. Berlin Philharmonic Orchestra. DGG LPM 18855; also in KL 27–31.

The English and the German performances took place about the same time in 1953. The English one was for this recording, while the German is taken from a concert in May of that year. I have stated elsewhere that there could hardly be more conclusive proof of Furtwängler's greatness of mind and spirit than these two performances. For both Menuhin and Schneiderhan, Furtwängler provides equally masterful, though entirely different, accompaniments to suit each violinist's approach. With Menuhin the orchestral part is more relaxed, the phrasing more flexible, and the interpretation oriented toward a more introspective and thoughtful reading. This is entirely in keeping with the Menuhin view, and the whole performance is a success. With Schneiderhan the handling is more forthright and vigorous, though never at the expense of subtlety, and Furtwängler brings out the march rhythms of the first movement more emphatically here, demonstrating that he was attuned to the needs of his soloists as much as to the requirements of the music. Either of these performances of the *Violin Concerto* would be a desirable one; to have both affords the opportunity for a fascinating study in comparative interpretation. Naturally the English recording, made under studio conditions, has the edge in sound, but the DGG version is perfectly acceptable. I must confess that my memory of the Lucerne performance is rather dim, but I do not remember it as being in the same class as the later Menuhin version, and certainly not as good as the Brahms *Violin Concerto* made about the same period. We do have the other two, and I list it here merely for the sake of completeness.

BRAHMS: *Symphony No. 1 in C minor, Op. 68*. Vienna Philharmonic Orchestra. HMV DB 6634-9; Electrola E 90992.

Although there are discs of the four Brahms symphonies, Furtwängler's Brahms is not as well represented on records as it should be. The *First* and *Second Symphonies* both stem from postwar 78 sets but, despite the supposed advantages of recording conditions over those pertaining to public performances, the former is slightly, the latter almost completely inadequate. The *First* opens with a startlingly ragged chord, which is followed by a rather sluggish first movement. From then on everything goes well, with a glowing Andante and a lilting Allegretto, the whole being crowned by a towering Finale whose majesty and nobility have rarely been so well conveyed on records. There is no slowing up for the brass chorale in the coda, which sweeps forward with tremendous vitality. The Electrola recording is a little uneasy in climaxes, but a French issue in the Great Recordings of the Century Series does have improved sound.

BRAHMS: *Symphony No. 2 in D, Op. 73*. London Philharmonic Orchestra. Decca K 1875-9; Ace of Clubs ACL 50; Richmond 19020.

Certainly almost anything would give a better idea of the *Second* than this London version. Anyone unfamiliar with Furtwängler's mastery would gain but a scant impression of it from this performance, which is ill-played and poorly recorded. It is surprising that Furtwängler passed it. The absence of an acceptable performance of the Brahms *Second* is one of the great lacunae of the Furtwängler discography. A Vienna performance was taped and indeed got as far as being pressed on disc, but has never been publicly released. A number awaits it in the Electrola catalogue (E 90993), but it is presumably held up for contractual reasons—a disgraceful situation. However, if it should prove impossible to secure this

198

version, a Berlin one of February 1953 should make an acceptable record.

BRAHMS: *Symphony No. 3 in F, Op. 90*. Berlin Philharmonic Orchestra. Electrola E 90994.

In this symphony, Furtwängler achieves a wonderful balance between the lyrical and dramatic aspects of the music. The middle two movements are set off against and contrasted with the outer ones. The Andante becomes a restful postscript to the arch-like, towering structure of the Allegro con brio, and the delicate Poco allegretto a preparation for the stormy Finale. In the first movement Furtwängler makes the all-important repeat which adds weight and depth to the composer's design. In the Finale it is even possible to suggest that Furtwängler is too fiery and hectic, but one is simply swept away by the fervour of the performance. The sound is acceptable, though it is surprising that the April 1954 performance in Berlin was not chosen. The five-year difference in techniques would have made some improvement.

BRAHMS: *Symphony No. 4 in E minor, Op. 98*. Berlin Philharmonic Orchestra. Electrola E 90995.

The *Fourth Symphony* is an equally impressive achievement. Furtwängler's appreciation of form and content here is rarely achieved by other conductors. Too often design is sacrificed for expressiveness or emotion forced into a rigid framework of formal cut; but Furtwängler obtains an ideal synthesis, symphonic strength being combined with expressive content in justly aligned proportions. Each movement is accorded its true weight in the scheme of things: thus the nobility of the second is realized with forceful dignity, the third presses forward with buoyant good humour, and the Passacaglia takes its place as the supreme edifice of Brahms's symphonic thought.

Brahms: *Violin Concerto*. Yehudi Menuhin, soloist. Lucerne Festival Orchestra. HMV DB 21000–4; Electrola E 90013.

Furtwängler recorded the Beethoven *Concerto* twice with Menuhin, the Brahms only once. It is open to doubt whether they could have surpassed this achievement, for it is a masterly account of the score, with soloist and conductor in complete harmony both as regards the intentions of the music and how they may best be attained. Apart from the interest in Furtwängler's shaping of the orchestral part, I know of no other recording which presents Menuhin in such commanding form, both technically and musically. He steers an admirable middle course between the lyrical and dramatic aspects of the music, bringing out the best of both, and the fiery rhythms of the Finale are thrilling. Menuhin is much helped by Furtwängler's adroit handling of the accompaniment, for he reveals the beauty of Brahms's orchestration as well as the work's masterly construction. The LP transfer is one of the best I have heard. The sound is wonderfully alive and detailed, and the quality in general astonishingly spacious for its age. To complete the picture, we ought really to have a version of the Brahms *Violin Concerto* conducted by Furtwängler in which the soloist is Schneiderhan, but the only possibility from Berlin seems to be a 1944 performance, and it is not to be supposed that, should a wire recording or tape exist, the sound could match this.

Bruckner: *Symphony No.9 in D minor*. Berlin Philharmonic Orchestra. DGG LPM 18854; also in KL 27–31.

Here, if anywhere, one would expect to find the "theory" of Furtwängler's slow tempi proved conclusively, but the sweep and fire of this volcanic performance shows that his understanding of Bruckner's essential cogency was all-embracing. The first movement is full of tension and has a cumulative impact which results from a sure grasp of the form and content. The Scherzo blazes with divine fire, while the Adagio has all its elegiac, heartbreaking qualities revealed to the full. All through Furtwängler displays a rare feeling for Bruckner's inventive orchestration and harmonies, and demonstrates that, far from being a conservative, hidebound traditionalist, Bruckner was one of the true innovators in orchestral writing. The recording, taken from a 1944 public performance, could have been wider in range, but it is amazing how much detail comes through. This is one of the essential Furtwängler discs, and it captures much of the passion of his live performances, as well as a fine interpretation of a noble work. At this writing, I have not heard test pressings of the *Seventh* and *Eighth Symphonies* scheduled for release by Electrola. They originate from postwar concerts with the Berlin Philharmonic.

CHERUBINI: *Anacreon Overture*. Vienna Philharmonic Orchestra. HMV DB 21493; HMV ALP 1498 (del.); Electrola E 70361; Electrola E 90152.

A marvelously moulded account of this fine piece marred by a very poor recording. The 78 was muffled and distant, the LP distorted badly towards the end. I have not heard the Electrola edition, but knowing what success the firm has had with other more difficult tasks in transferring 78s to LP, it could well be the most acceptable. The Vienna string playing alone is enough to make this an essential acquisition.

FRANCK: *Symphony in D minor*. Vienna Philharmonic Orchestra. Decca LXT 2905 (del.); Ace of Clubs ACL 179; London CM 9091; Eurodisc 70368 KK.

Decca once announced that it had Furtwängler under contract, but he died before much of significance could be accomplished. All that was recorded was the Franck *Symphony*, by no means my favourite work. Furtwängler's ennobling influence does actually raise the work to the status of sounding like inferior Brahms. The opening of the Finale is quite impressive, but all the care lavished on the performance, and it is clearly a very great deal, cannot make me attend to the music. For the most part Furtwängler's keen sense of structure makes the work seem shorter than usual, and for those who wish it, here is the Franck given the kind of superior performance not likely to recur. The Ace of Clubs transfer is weighty and full, with impressive brass. The newer Eurodisc I have not heard, but it presumably differs little.

FURTWÄNGLER: *Symphony No. 2 in E minor*. Berlin Philharmonic Orchestra. DGG LPM 18114–5.

In honor of the tenth anniversary of Furtwängler's death, DGG is planning a reissue of his *Second Symphony*, which he recorded with his Berlin musicians in the early fifties. It has been unavailable for some time.

HAYDN: *Symphony No. 88 in G*. SCHUMANN: *Symphony No. 4 in D minor*. Berlin Philharmonic Orchestra. DGG LPM 18858; Heliodor DG 478146; also in KL 27–31.

These two performances have gone through so many transformations that they must despair of ever settling down to an orderly existence. The Haydn, a recording of December 1951, was originally the fourth side of the Schubert *Ninth*, and in addition to being coupled with the Schumann work, it has also been linked with the Mozart 39 on LPM 18725. The Schumann was originally issued on a 10-inch disc by itself and is still available in Germany in that form on LPE 17170. Both performances are outstanding. The Schumann in fact is a revelation of just how fine a work it can sound. Furtwängler misses none of the music's Romantic warmth, its tenderness and its glow. The coda to the Finale leaves one breathless with excitement, and the tense handling of the transition between the third and fourth movements has one on the edge of the chair. The Haydn is a quite exceptional account, with the crisp tempi and alert rhythms in the outer movements wonderfully invigorating, while the eloquent reading of the sublime Largo takes one into the heart of Haydn. The orchestral playing is responsive and ardent, with superb string work in the Largo. The recordings now sound very well, a pitch wobble on early pressings of the Haydn having been eliminated.

HAYDN: *Symphony No.94 in G, "Surprise"*. Vienna Philharmonic Orchestra. HMV ALP 1011 (del.); Electrola E 91075.

Since in the Electrola pressing this performance is coupled with the marvelous Mozart No.40, and since it is the only other recording of a Haydn symphony by Furtwängler, this record is a must. Once again his sense of Classical form, his feeling for line and rhythmic articulation (just listen to the Minuet and the lively Finale!), and his realization of the true power that lies behind Haydn's music mark out Furtwängler as one of the finest Haydn conductors of the century. The recording still sounds excellent in the Electrola transfer, reproducing the well-proportioned performance with admirable clarity. There is too little of Furtwängler's Haydn on records for a composer he played so much; there ought to be more, and perhaps the *Clock Symphony* of 1947 would be a start.

HINDEMITH: *Symphonic Metamorphosis on Themes of Weber*. Berlin Philharmonic Orchestra. DGG LPM 18857.

Furtwängler's staunch championship of Hindemith is well known, and not even the composer himself puts this work in so attractive a light. In this performance the music has a rare sparkle, and Furtwängler exhorts his orchestra to superb feats of virtuosity. Here, too, he displays a sense of colour and texture that brings greater clarity to Hindemith's normally complex textures, and there is a surprising amount of detail in this 1947 recording. The performance refutes the suggestion that Furtwängler had no feeling for or sympathy with modern music, for it takes considerable insight to bring the best out of music of any period, and here Furtwängler shows an unmatched realization of the composer's intentions. More Hindemith from Furtwängler, such as the *Harmonie der Welt* world première of 1952, would be valuable.

Liszt: *Les Préludes*. Vienna Philharmonic Orchestra. HMV ALP 1220 (del.); Electrola E 90097; Electrola E 60661.

This is a magnificent example of Furtwängler's ability to take an inferior piece and ennoble it to undreamt-of heights. Perhaps the results here are almost too noble, but the effect is of overwhelming grandeur. One may regret that the time was not better spent, but we can only be grateful for the results, even if we can never expect to hear *Les Préludes* played like this again. The recording is excellent.

Mahler: *Lieder eines fahrenden Gesellen*. Dietrich Fischer-Dieskau, soloist. Philharmonia Orchestra. HMV ALP 1270; Electrola E 90106; Angel 35522.

Fischer-Dieskau made his Salzburg début in 1951 singing this cycle with the Vienna Philharmonic under Furtwängler. That was a performance to treasure, but so even more is this recording which shows everyone at peak form. Furtwängler probes so deeply into the essence of the work's meaning and displays such a profound understanding of the composer's idiom that one is left amazed and baffled that he did not record much more Mahler than he did. The heartfelt grief at the end of the last song is as poignant in its beauty in the orchestra as it is in Fischer-Dieskau's magical handling of the vocal line. Furtwängler's tempi, though by no means traditional, always sound right, and he draws playing of great expressiveness from the Philharmonia. As the rare instance of Furtwängler and Mahler this performance is invaluable. It has recently been deleted in Britain, but I understand it is to be reissued with Fischer-Dieskau's first recording of the *Kindertotenlieder*. It would be much more to the point were it to be reissued with the Fischer-Dieskau/Furtwängler *Kindertotenlieder* performance given in Berlin in December 1953.

MENDELSSOHN: *Midsummer Night's Dream Overture*. Berlin Philharmonic Orchestra. Polydor 66925-6; reissued DGG 69206-7 (del.).

I cannot understand why this performance has not so far been reissued on LP or even EP. It is surely one of the classic accounts of this most enchanting of overtures. The string playing at the opening is of ethereal, delicate lightness, and the earthy episodes spring naturally out of the context rather than appear to be imposed upon it as is so often the case. It certainly makes one wish that Furtwängler had recorded more of this music. Failing a reissue of this, the Berlin performance of September 1947 should be investigated to see whether an acceptable recording can be made.

MENDELSSOHN: *Hebrides Overture*. Berlin Philharmonic Orchestra. Polydor 95470; Decca CA 8090 (del.). Vienna Philharmonic Orchestra. HMV DB 6941; HMV ALP 1526 (del.); Electrola E 60655.

Neither of these performances is currently available in British pressings, but it is to be hoped that the HMV will appear again, perhaps under more dignified auspices than "Furtwängler Pop Concert", as the LP was called. The sea throbs and pulsates evocatively in both versions, but the Vienna performance is at once more profound and grander. Here, too, the better recording is a positive advantage, and it was well transferred in its LP format.

MENDELSSOHN: *Violin Concerto*. Yehudi Menuhin, soloist. Berlin Philharmonic Orchestra. HMV ALP 1135; Electrola E 60546. BEETHOVEN: *Violin Romances Nos. 1 and 2*. Yehudi Menuhin, soloist. Philharmonia Orchestra. HMV ALP 1135; Electrola E 50513.

It seems easiest to consider these performances together at this point, but I must confess that I do not have any great enthusiasm for the record. As usual, the Menuhin/Furtwängler collaboration works wonders with the music, and if one would ideally prefer more flashing pyrotechnics to make the Mendelssohn more palatable and less wearisome than it always appears, there is much to be said for the persuasive charm which Menuhin brings to the music. Even Furtwängler cannot do much towards making the accompaniment sound more interesting than it is, but there are inevitably moments of character which one does not often find. The Beethoven *Romances* are played with a stylistic expressiveness that temporarily makes the music sound more meaningful than it really is, and Furtwängler provides a worthy accompaniment. The recording itself is all that could be desired.

MOZART: *The Abduction from the Seraglio Overture. The Marriage of Figaro Overture*. Berlin Philharmonic Orchestra. Polydor 35013; reissued DGG EPL 30172 (45 rpm).

This is a useful reissue of performances from the early thirties, but hardly adequate in preserving for us an example of Furtwängler's way with Mozart operas. The beautiful development of the *Figaro Overture* shows how rewarding a complete performance must have been, and it should surely be possible to find an acceptable tape of one of the postwar Salzburg presentations. *The Abduction* is sprightly and good-humoured, and the sound fine.

MOZART: *Serenade No. 10 in B flat, K. 361*. Vienna Philharmonic Wind Ensemble. HMV DB 6707–11; Electrola E 91175.

This was clearly a labour of love, for rarely has there been a recording in which the conductor's affection for and understanding of the music so patently shines through every bar. Furtwängler shows so complete a comprehension of the style as to make most other performances seem perfunctory and ephemeral. He plumbs the depths of the Variations, drawing sounds of ravishing beauty from his players, and reveals the poignant heartache of the Romanze, while the high spirits of the Finale are boisterously captured. The allegro of the first movement is, if anything, possibly on the fast side, but it has a captivating enthusiasm that disarms. The thirteen players are completely at Furtwängler's command, and the tonal magic of the sound could only be produced by Viennese artists at their most inspired. The recording was made under difficult circumstances in Vienna during one of its coldest winters shortly after the war, but the quality is generally satisfactory, and the LP transfer has been well carried out. Only one or two slight patches of roughness betray its origins. Nevertheless it would have to be very poor indeed to prevent one from realizing that here is one of the great Mozart recordings of all time.

MOZART: *Serenade No. 13 in G, K. 525, "Eine kleine Nachtmusik"*. Berlin Philharmonic Orchestra. Polydor 67156–8; reissued DGG EPL 30576 (45 rpm). Vienna Philharmonic Orchestra. HMV DB 6911–2; HMV ALP 1498 (del.); Electrola E 60543.

Almost every conductor seems to have to record this work; only Toscanini appears to have escaped, and Furtwängler underwent the ordeal twice. There is little to choose between the two. Perhaps the Berlin performance shows a shade more nuance and flexibility in the phrasing, with just a touch more graciousness in the Minuet, but it is a moot point. The transfer is good, with a remarkably faithful string tone. The Vienna performance is more resonantly recorded, and there is some blurring of detail. The Electrola 10-inch disc seems to be the only way to obtain this performance now. If on neither recording of the *Eine kleine* does Furtwängler's imagination appear to have been fully exercised, one can hardly be too surprised.

MOZART: *Symphony No. 39 in E flat, K. 543*. Berlin Philharmonic Orchestra. DGG LPM 18725; DGG LPM 18856; also in KL 27–31.

This and the *G minor* are the only Mozart symphonies of which Furtwängler recordings exist. There would not seem to be any Berlin tapes which could provide others, and we can only regretfully look back to the prewar concerts which show both the *Prague* and the *Jupiter Symphonies*. This *E flat* is a wartime performance, and the first thing one notices is the strength of line. No matter how malleable the phrasing becomes for the purposes of expression, the underlying pulse is never lost or neglected, and one is made newly aware of the grandeur of Mozart's construction. One could hardly fault the interpretation, certainly not for the way Furtwängler brings out the Romantic undertones of the score. A performance of this caliber shows how far advanced Mozart was along the path to Romanticism. I could wish for a better recording, however. The sound is bottom-heavy, with thumping tympani and a generally thick quality, but the stature of the interpretation is evident.

MOZART: *Symphony No. 40 in G minor, K. 550*. Vienna Philharmonic Orchestra. HMV DB 6997–9; HMV ALP 1498 (del.); Electrola E 91075; Electrola E 70361.

Furtwängler is the only conductor, apart from Fritz Reiner on his early Pittsburgh recording, to give proper value to the tempo marking of the first movement. Despite some indications to the contrary, it is a Molto allegro, i.e. very fast, and it is only at

Furtwängler's pacing that the music emerges with anything like its true force and strength. He shapes the opening phrase in one single arch so that forward momentum is immediately established and one is carried away by the music. Tension is not relaxed for the second subject, and so great is the drama that one can fully appreciate, as if for the first time, the deep emotion and stark power of the symphony. The Andante is heart-rendingly poignant and the firm tread of the Minuet is superbly etched in. The Finale, again taken at a proper speed, is also imbued with true Mozartian strength. Other performances, particularly Bruno Walter's, may offer different aspects of this enigmatic symphony in greater measure, but none gives so much of the music. The Electrola pressing has rich sound.

ROSSINI: *Il Barbiere di Siviglia Overture*. Berlin Philharmonic Orchestra. Polydor 35028; Decca CA 8218 (del.). *La Gazza Ladra Overture*. Berlin Philharmonic Orchestra. Polydor 95427; Decca CA 8055 (del.).

These are the only recordings of any Rossini by Furtwängler, and indeed, some people may be surprised to find that they exist at all. Contemporary accounts of his early career indicate that he had quite a flair for Italian opera, and though he concentrated upon more serious works in later years, Furtwängler evidently had great feeling for buffo style. Certainly these two performances are as lively and as pointed as one could wish; the superbly judged crescendi in *La Gazza Ladra* are sufficient proof of Furtwängler's command of the idiom. The horn playing in the *Barber* is marvelously liquid, and the Berlin Philharmonic gives the impression that it has never done anything else but play Italian opera. I am not aware of any public performances which would provide something of Rossini in more up-to-date sound, but failing that, these should certainly be resuscitated.

SCHUBERT: *Symphony No. 8 in B minor, D.759, "Unfinished"*. Vienna Philharmonic Orchestra. HMV DB 21131–3 (del.); Electrola E 60550.

Recorded in 1950, this is the only Furtwängler *Unfinished* on disc, apart from his rehearsal of the opening bars with the Berlin Philharmonic on the Period record "The Berlin Philharmonic Plays" (SPL 716). Furtwängler here brings out the brooding, ominous qualities of the score; the opening of the first movement is barely audible, but the basic pulse is there, and the underlying momentum is carried through without loss of tension or slackening of dramatic effect. Notice, too, how the rhythm of the tympani in the Andante is firmly maintained, and the effective contrast that is drawn between the two thematic groups. There are other ways of playing the *Unfinished* which are just as valid as this one, but Furtwängler's is as convincing as any, and perhaps a little more truly Schubertian than most. The recording is a little thin at times, and there is a curious hollowness about the sound in climaxes, but it is always acceptable and the greatness of the performance comes through.

SCHUBERT: *Symphony No. 9 in C, D.944, "The Great"*. Berlin Philharmonic Orchestra. DGG LPM 18015–6 (del.); DGG LPM 18347; Heliodor DGM 18347; also in KL 27–31.

It is generally agreed, even by those who are normally anti-Furtwängler, that this contains one of his very best performances. It has held its place at the head of the long list of recordings of this work for more than ten years, and no other version has succeeded in surpassing it, though there are accounts which can be placed on the same level. Curiously enough, one of these comes from the conductor most often cited as the complete antithesis to Furtwängler, Toscanini. It must be stressed, however, that this comparison applies only when the Italian's Philadelphia version is considered; his others are not of the same quality. Both men achieve their results through different means. Toscanini emphasizes rhythm and strictness of tempo; Furtwängler, while not neglecting either of these attributes, delves more deeply into the score, and by the plastic continuity of his phrasing brings out the magic of the music. It is in the Andante that Furtwängler leaves his rivals standing. Even Toscanini saw the need for some variation in tempo here, and Furtwängler, by letting the music unfold, takes one into the very heart and soul of the composer. The last two movements leave nothing to be desired in matters of rhythmic propulsion and sonorously built climaxes, while the Scherzo shows that Furtwängler could handle a symphonic dance movement with a real appreciation of its mood. The two live performances of the *C major* by Furtwängler that I remember were both with the Vienna Philharmonic, and though the splendour of sound of those events seems a little closer, the performances were by no means superior to this Berlin one. The orchestra plays magnificently; the superb ease and confidence of the brass is a constant joy. The recording was originally spread over three sides, which gave the music room to breathe. The later pressing was somewhat cramped and the dynamic range seemed limited in comparison with the two-record set. The best results of all are to be obtained from the transfer in the Memorial Album (KL 27–31).

SCHUMANN: *Manfred Overture, Op. 115.* Vienna Philharmonic Orchestra. HMV BLP 1009 (del.); Electrola E 60661.

This is the kind of performance whose excellence one forgets until one plays it again. I should expect Furtwängler to excel in this powerfully Romantic music, and he does not disappoint. For him Romanticism was no hazy dream, but a strong, bold, forthright movement, full of strength and ardour, and this is the way he plays *Manfred*. The reading has drama, fervour and impact, with a colourful realization of all the music's elements. The Electrola pressing with its vibrantly immediate strings is a great improvement on the early HMV disc. This and the *Fourth Symphony* are the only Furtwängler recordings of Schumann. There may be wire recordings of the *Cello Concerto* from 1942 and 1943, which does not matter, and the *Piano Concerto* which appeared twice on his Berlin programs in 1942, once with Gieseking and once with Cortot, which does. There is also a Vienna Philharmonic performance of the *First Symphony* on tape, and possibly other Schumann works led by Furtwängler have been preserved.

SMETANA: *Vltava*. Vienna Philharmonic Orchestra. HMV BLP 1015 (del.); Electrola E 60543.

This is very much *Die Moldau* rather than *Vltava*. Furtwängler's performance is weighty and majestic, and even the opening lacks the lightness of touch one normally expects to find. Yet if one accepts the approach, the interpretation is not without charm, and the final episode is full of dignified power. The recording is not one of the best of the Vienna series, however, and climaxes tend to sound rough.

JOHANN STRAUSS: *Die Fledermaus Overture*. Berlin Philharmonic Orchestra. Polydor 67121 (del.). *Emperor Waltz, Op. 437*. Vienna Philharmonic Orchestra. HMV DB 21174; HMV ALP 1526 (del.); Electrola 7 RF 148 (45 rpm).

I have been unable to hear the *Fledermaus*, since not even the BBC library possessed a copy. I can only plead for a DGG reissue so that my curiosity can be appeased. One does not normally associate the world of Johann Strauss with Furtwängler, though I recall a broadcast which had several delectable polkas and waltzes, but this performance of the *Emperor Waltz* shows that his stylistic sympathies extended more widely than is usually suspected. The introduction is appropriately formal and dignified, with a marvelously pompous (in its right sense) stride, and the lilting of the waltz chain has unforgettable force. This is arguably the greatest of Strauss's waltzes, and Furtwängler does it full justice, showing a true appreciation of its stature. The recording is a little tight, but there is enough tonal bloom for this not to matter too much. It should be made available on LP again.

JOSEF STRAUSS: *Pizzicato Polka*. Vienna Philharmonic Orchestra. HMV DB 21173; HMV ALP 1526 (del.); Electrola 7 RF 148 (45 rpm).

Although the rhythm is firm and stylish, Furtwängler's pacing is perhaps a little deliberate here. It sounds a trifle like an exercise in technical control, and though one can enjoy the results there is a slight loss of charm. The string tone is solid and warm, and the record does deserve LP reissue as one of Furtwängler's rare Strauss Family recordings.

RICHARD STRAUSS: *Don Juan, Op. 20*. Vienna Philharmonic Orchestra. HMV ALP 1208 (del.); Electrola E 70429.

In some ways, this is the finest of all Furtwängler recordings of Richard Strauss's works, for he brings out the sensuality of the score in an unequalled manner. The interpretation accents the intensity of the Don's search, but does not ignore the undeniable fact that the search is also a source of pleasure. Where many other conductors concentrate on the sheer physical excitement of the music, Furtwängler reveals the longing and the striving that underlie the score. The playing and recording are both excellent, the mono sound having considerable vitality in spite of its ten years. It would be better to have this combined with *Till Eulenspiegel* and *Tod und Verklärung* on one record, but for now the Electrola issue is a good one to have.

RICHARD STRAUSS: *Metamorphosen*. Berlin Philharmonic Orchestra. DGG LPM 18857.

Another work eminently suited to the Furtwängler approach. Perhaps the performance is a little too saturated with grief and the final effect rather too elegiac and mournful, but the passion and sincerity of the reading still one's doubts, and the marvelous tone Furtwängler conjures from the Berlin strings must be close to what the composer had in mind. The work is undoubtedly one of Strauss's masterpieces, and the recording is satisfying even though one cannot help longing for the greater clarity that stereo would bring.

RICHARD STRAUSS: *Till Eulenspiegels lustige Streiche, Op. 28*. Berlin Philharmonic Orchestra. Polydor 95410–1; Decca CA 8053–4 (del.). Berlin Philharmonic Orchestra. DGG ELP 30589. Vienna Philharmonic Orchestra. HMV ALP 1208 (del.); Electrola E 70429.

The position regarding the Furtwängler recordings of *Till* is already complicated enough without citing the fact that there was another Berlin performance which appeared on Period SPL 716, made from the sound track of Ambassador Films's *Symphony* in 1952. The 78s were on three sides, with a devastating account of Berlioz's *Rakóczy March* on the fourth, and the lithe strength of Furtwängler's interpretation still comes through the faded sound. He revels in Till's activities, and rarely has the character emerged in so flamboyant a fashion. This is a rogue who does not care about the consequences of his deeds, and there is clearly no repentance in his final leave-taking. The later performances are a little more considered, but the Vienna one has a truly shattering climax. The Berlin version is a bit hectic by comparison, but the orchestra seems to follow the conductor with greater intensity.

RICHARD STRAUSS: *Tod und Verklärung, Op. 24*. Vienna Philharmonic Orchestra. Pathé Marconi FALP 546.

A profound and deeply philosophical performance to which the recording does not do justice. Perhaps an Electrola transfer would improve this, but one is still able to discern the quality of the interpretation through the somewhat murky sound of this French issue, the only one at present available. One would expect this work to suit Furtwängler's temperament, and he does convey its essential mystery and sense of struggle.

TCHAIKOVSKY: *Symphony No. 4 in F minor, Op. 36.* Vienna Philharmonic Orchestra. HMV ALP 1025 (del.); Encore ENC 109; Electrola E 90030.

The finely-wrought imagination which makes Furtwängler's *Pathétique* so fascinating is in evidence here, even if at times it seems to be slightly studied in application. The dramatic episodes have the commanding fire one seeks, but some of the linking passages, notably the lead into the first allegro, are just a shade deliberate. The plaintive oboe solo at the beginning of the slow movement is beautifully phrased, and the string playing is of characteristic warmth. The Scherzo is perfectly interpreted as a point of contrast between the poignancy of the Andante and the violence of the Finale. The Finale itself blazes forth with unremitting splendour, and if the total effect is not quite as overwhelming as the performance deserves to be, this is undoubtedly the fault of the recording. The Encore pressing tends to tonal thinness and a lack of body in heavy brass and lower strings; however, it is certainly serviceable, and there does not appear to be a public performance late enough to offer a tape which would produce anything better. A Berlin performance of the *Fifth* in October 1947 might yield a suitable tape. It would be welcome on discs as a completion of the last three Tchaikovsky symphonies conducted by Furtwängler.

TCHAIKOVSKY: *Symphony No. 6 in B minor, Op. 74, "Pathétique".* Berlin Philharmonic Orchestra. HMV DB 4609–14; Electrola E 91079; Angel COLH 21.

If I were forced to cite just one Furtwängler interpretation to prove his greatness, I think my choice would fall on this one. This is not simply a case of taking a lesser work and making it sound great, but of taking a great work and realizing its true strength and integrity in an incomparable manner. The *Pathétique* may sometimes seem a hackneyed work, and in the average run of performances it is, but this is not the average run. Furtwängler takes the work and by concentrating upon its musical values he restores Tchaikovsky's symphonic masterpiece its true stature. No one has equalled Furtwängler in the second movement, whose grace and charm are brought out with wonderful elegance, while the fire of the March is possibly approached only by Fricsay, working with the same orchestra in later years, though Furtwängler strikes incredible power from the coda. But it is the moving dignity of the Finale which crowns this reading, as Furtwängler distils the music's tragic essence with a simplicity and an emotion that is all the more touching for not being overtly stated. The nobility of this performance makes one realize how unjustly Tchaikovsky is generally treated. The playing of the Berlin Philharmonic is absolutely dedicated to the fulfillment of Furtwängler's intentions, and not a point is lost. The 78s produced a remarkable sound for their day, and the LP transfers faithfully reproduce their clarity and presence.

WAGNER: *Götterdämmerung. Dawn and Siegfried's Rhine Journey.* Vienna Philharmonic Orchestra. HMV DB 6949–50; HMV ALP 1016; Electrola E 90026. *Siegfried's Funeral Music.* Berlin Philharmonic Orchestra. Polydor 67054; Decca CA 8173 (del.). Vienna Philharmonic Orchestra. HMV DB 6946; HMV ALP 1016;

Electrola E 90026. *Brünnhilde's Immolation and Closing Scene*. Kirsten Flagstad, soloist. Philharmonia Orchestra. HMV DB 6792–4; later version, HMV ALP 1016; Electrola E 90026.

The LP issue contains different performances from the 78s. The combination of Flagstad and Furtwängler in the *Immolation Scene* is unequalled; certainly no other performance I have heard is as unfailingly majestic and moving as this one. The *Dawn* and *Rhine Journey* are superbly evocative, and the *Funeral Music* represents a cosmic collapse. This is not just the death of a hero, but the end of Valhalla and all it stands for. The climax is shattering. The 78s are important documents, but the LP is one of the great records of all time. In recent pressings it sounds tremendous.

WAGNER: *Lohengrin, Prelude to Act I*. Berlin Philharmonic Orchestra. Polydor 95408; reissued DGG 95408 (del.). Vienna Philharmonic Orchestra. HMV ALP 1220 (del.); Electrola E 90097; Electrola E 91074.

I list the 78 rpm version for the sake of completeness; although it is a finely sensitive account, it is clearly surpassed by the LP. The Vienna orchestra produces some ravishing string tone, and this was one of the best recordings Furtwängler was accorded in Vienna.

WAGNER: *Tristan and Isolde, Prelude and Liebestod*. Berlin Philharmonic Orchestra. Polydor 95438–9; *Liebestod* only, reissued DGG ELP 30540 (45 rpm). Berlin Philharmonic Orchestra. HMV DB 3419–20.

The Polydor set, from 1930, does indeed sound a little dim, but the reissued *Liebestod* gives far greater clarity. The HMV set, made some years later but still before the war, was a classic of its day, and it is to be reissued soon in the Great Recordings of the Century Series, together with Furtwängler's eloquent reading of the *Prelude and Good Friday Spell* from *Parsifal*, made during the same period. Incomparable playing from the Berlin Philharmonic marks these sets, and the sound from the 78s still glows. The only Berlin concert performance of the *Tristan* music dates from April 1954; the tape of this might well be considered for publication.

WAGNER: *Tristan and Isolde*. Kirsten Flagstad (Isolde), Ludwig Suthaus (Tristan), Blanche Thebom (Brangaene), Dietrich Fischer-Dieskau (Kurwenal), Josef Greindl (King Mark), Rudolf Schock (Seaman, Shepherd), Edgar Evans (Melot), Roderick Davis (Steersman). Philharmonia Orchestra and Chorus of the Royal Opera House, Covent Garden. HMV ALP 1030–5; Electrola E 91170–4; Angel 3588–E/1. *Highlights*. Electrola E 80712–3.

It is sometimes forgotten that Furtwängler, like almost all the great Central European conductors, began his career in the opera house, and that throughout his active musical life he continued to conduct opera as much as orchestral music. His repertory was much broader than it is generally held to have been, taking in such widely separated works as *Carmen* and *Otello* and giving memorable performances of both. Certainly this *Tristan* is the almost perfect memorial to his greatness as an operatic conductor, and one scarcely knows where to begin in selecting its praiseworthy points. It is not just the majestic sweep of the first-act Finale, the sensuality and eroticism of the Love Duet, nor the heart-rending lament of Tristan's third-act monologue and the soul-searing tragedy of the *Liebestod* that make this performance have such an overwhelming effect, but the utter and complete identification of everyone concerned with the music itself. The listener becomes involved with the drama and is swept up by the suffusing emotions of the work. It is impossible to hear this performance dispassionately. Under the inspiring guidance of Furtwängler, Flagstad is an expressive Isolde, and she is well supported by Suthaus. Fischer-

Dieskau in his first operatic recording is a forthright Kurwenal, and all the other roles are well sung. The sound is impressive, and all the up-to-date splendour of stereo could not suffice to remove from this recording the description "irreplaceable".

WAGNER: *Die Walküre*. Leonie Rysanek (Sieglinde), Martha Mödl (Brünnhilde), Margarete Klose (Fricka), Ludwig Suthaus (Sieg-mund), Ferdinand Frantz (Wotan), Gottlob Frick (Hunding), Gerda Scheyrer, Judith Hellwig, Dagmar Schmedes, Ruth Siewert, Erika Köth, Hertha Töpper, Johanna Blatter, Dagmar Hermann (Valkyries). Vienna Philharmonic Orchestra. HMV ALP 1257–61; Electrola E 90100–4.

It is no secret that HMV was planning to record the entire *Ring* under Furtwängler, a project which, if completed, would have stood as an enduring monument of our time. It is also no secret that Kirsten Flagstad did not sing the role of Brünnhilde here because she was incensed at the revelation by the company that she did not sing two notes in the complete *Tristan* recording. It is doubly unfortunate in that Mödl's Brünnhilde is the weakest part of the set, for she does not sustain the bright shining tones that are almost a *sine qua non* of the Valkyrie Brünnhilde. There is no doubting her intelligence and understanding of the role, as her moving contribution to the *Todesverkündigung* shows, but sheer vocal command and stamina are lacking. Ferdinand Frantz is a fine Wotan, not as imposing as Hotter, but his lighter voice is clean and clearly focussed, and he is no less eloquent in the Farewell than some more renowned exponents of the role. Frick is a sono-rous Hunding; Klose, who recorded Fricka on 78s before the war, brings her rich voice and long experience to the part with reward-ing effect. Rysanek is a radiant Sieglinde, this being one of her finest performances on records; and Suthaus is a strong, if not ideally free, Siegmund. But over it all strides the gigantic figure of Furtwängler. Here again "magisterial" is the word for his work. His conducting has passion, atmosphere, drama and sustained tension so that the opera unfolds Wagner's vision fully. From the opening storm to the final leave-taking, every phrase and theme is moulded into the grand design, with every dramatic and musical point made. The Vienna Philharmonic provides what is perhaps its greatest playing for Furtwängler on records, and the recording itself does all that one could wish in conveying Furtwängler's profound comprehension of the opera. Even though we are to have the complete *Ring* from the 1953 Radio Italiana performances led by Furtwängler, it is unlikely that the *Walküre* will surpass this one.

Weber: *Der Freischütz Overture* and *Prelude to Act III*. Berlin Philharmonic Orchestra. Polydor 67108–9; Decca CA 8262–3 (del.). *Overture* only. Vienna Philharmonic Orchestra. LHMV 19 (del.).

Der Freischütz was one of Furtwängler's great loves, and it was at his insistence that the Salzburg Festival mounted it for him in 1954. Ideally tapes of the complete performance should be released on records, for, although some of the singing was below par, orchestrally it was unforgettable. Furtwängler achieved the most enchanting of effects in the Bridesmaids' Chorus, where one would have thought that lace bows on silken strings would be necessary to obtain the incredible delicacy of the performance. As it is, all we have is the *Overture* and, on the prewar discs, the third-act *Prelude*. This is a wonderfully evocative account, with magical horn playing and a vividly alive coda. The sound is still acceptable, and DGG should include it in a future reissue. As far as I know, the Vienna performance of the *Overture* has only appeared on the Victor HMV disc as a filler for *Till Eulenspiegel* and *Don Juan*. I cannot understand why this should be, for the recording is fine, and Furtwängler probes the Romantic depths of the music in a way that no one else can match, even if the pulse is a little less urgent than in the prewar set.

WEBER: *Euryanthe Overture*. Vienna Philharmonic Orchestra. LHMV 19 (del.).

Like the Vienna *Freischütz*, this performance has only appeared on the Strauss record just mentioned. It is a marvelous reading; the mysterious central section has never sounded more eerie, and the swing of the allegros is quite invigorating. These two performances deserve to be made more accessible.

WEBER: *Oberon Overture*. Vienna Philharmonic Orchestra. HMV DB 21104; HMV ALP 1526 (del.); Electrola E 60655.

This recording is a little unsteady in tone. It is perhaps the least successful of Furtwängler's Weber records, and though the introduction is wonderful and the atmosphere well caught, some of the expected fire is missing. However, the three Weber overtures would surely make one LP side, and HMV should look into it. In every area of Furtwängler's repertory, there is much to be done to give the public more documentation of his art.

PUBLICATIONS BY WILHELM FURTWÄNGLER

Compositions

Sonata for Violin and Piano. Edition Breitkopf 5668 (Leipzig, 1938; Wiesbaden, Breitkopf & Härtel).

Sonata No. 2 in D Major for Violin and Piano (Berlin, Bote & Bock, 1940).

Symphony No. 2 in E Minor. Study score, 325 pages; conductor's score, orchestral parts available on loan basis (Wiesbaden, Brucknerverlag, 1952).

Symphonic Concerto for Piano and Orchestra. Edition for two pianos, 97 pages (Wiesbaden, Brucknerverlag, 1955).

Books

Gespräche über Musik (Vienna, Humboldt Verlag, 1949; 2nd ed., Zürich and Freiburg i/Br., Atlantis Verlag, 1955). English edition translated by L.J.Lawrence, *Concerning Music* (London, Boosey & Hawkes, 1953).

Ton und Wort. Aufsätze und Vorträge 1918–1954 (Wiesbaden, F.A.Brockhaus Verlag, 1954). English edition translated by L.A.Fenn, *Collected Essays* (London, John Calder Publishers Limited, 1965).

Der Musiker und sein Publikum (Zürich and Freiburg i/Br., Atlantis Verlag, 1955).

Vermächtnis (Wiesbaden, F.A.Brockhaus Verlag, 1956).

Briefe (Wiesbaden, F.A.Brockhaus Verlag, 1964).

INDEX OF WRITERS

Photographic sources

1   Court Conductor in Mannheim, c. 1915. G. Tillmann-Matter, Mannheim

2   Vienna, 1930. Trude Fleischmann, New York

3, 4 Rehearsal in Vienna, 1944. Hans Reznichek, Vienna

5   After his last *Ninth* at Bayreuth, 1954. Haselhorst, Bielefeld

Cover photo by Rudolf Kessler, Berlin